OPTIMISM

for

AUTISM

OPTIMISM for AUTISM
Copyright © 2014 by Susan Jane King

First Edition

Bible references quoted in this book are from: BibleGateway. The Lockman Foundation, n.d. Web. <http://www.biblegateway.com/>.

Cover design: Narrow Way Design
Cover photography: Leslie Denton/Pura Vida Photography
Author photos: Karen Goforth/Irresistible Portraits

Printed in South Carolina, the United States of America

ISBN-13: 978-1495978432
ISBN-10: 1495978435

OPTIMISM

for

AUTISM

THE INSPIRATIONAL JOURNEY
OF A MOTHER AND HER AUTISTIC SON

BY SUSAN JANE KING
with Patrick King

DEDICATION

This book is dedicated to the Lord God Almighty—
"For great is the Lord and greatly to be praised."
—Psalm 96:4, NASB

From Susan:
I would also like to dedicate this book to my husband David—
warrior, soulmate, provider, protector—
who has skillfully led our family with both strength
and tenderness
on this magnificent journey.
I love and admire you with all my heart!

From Patrick:
I would also like to dedicate this book to my mom.
Thanks, Mom, for all the love and support you have
given me over the years.
You have helped me become the person I am today.

SUSAN JANE KING

CONTENTS

1

WHAT'S WRONG?

"Oh, my anguish, my anguish! I writhe in pain.
Oh, the agony of my heart!"
—Jeremiah 4:19, NIV

My ears pricked to the sound, like a rabbit that halts mid-nibble, tingling with the sense of impending danger. My brain quickly registered what my ears had heard.

Bam. Bam. Bam.

A signal rapidly traveled from my brain to my legs. *Run!*

Laundry scattered as I dropped the basket. My heart was racing as I sped down the steps. *I have to be fast! I've got to get to him, before . . .*

My ears strained to follow the direction of the sound. I rounded the corner into the kitchen, and there he was, my precious two-year-old son, violently pounding his head into the hardwood floor.

I grabbed him, adrenaline producing a rapid yank. His body jerked into a stiff, wooden form the instant I touched him, as if a powerful electrical shock had moved from my arms and zig-zagged its way over his small frame. He looked past me, distant and aloof.

I was too late.

Blood had already started trickling down the side of his face. That sweet face which couldn't tolerate my kisses.

Now it was my time to bleed.

I felt the familiar trickle work its way down my heart.

What is wrong with my son?

I knew this wasn't normal. His three sisters had never acted like this. By the time they had turned 3, they were busy chatting, playing tea party, and doling out lots of hugs and kisses to their mommy and daddy. I sat there, rocking my little bundle of agony, as he stared off into space.

It had all started with such promise . . .

The ultrasound wand slid through the sticky gel that had been smoothed across my belly. My husband David and I strained to see if we could make sense of the varying hues of gray on the screen. We had three delightful daughters, ages 1, 3, and 5, and though we loved our girls, we secretly hoped the Lord would allow us the blessing and adventure of raising a boy. My husband grew up the youngest of three brothers, all two years apart. Memories of building forts in the woods, playing pickup games of basketball, and camping outdoors etched their places into his collective memory. He and I hoped he would have the opportunity to raise a son and do all those things with him.

"It's a boy!" the ultrasound technician announced.

The room was dark, but I saw the tear glide down my husband's cheek.

We anticipated Patrick's arrival with joy. We chose to name him after his great uncle Patrick Rebillot, a gifted jazz pianist who moved to New York City as a young adult and made a name for himself in the music industry. I was drawn to my Uncle Pat at a young age, enthralled by his gentle nature, wisdom, and quick sense of humor. When he played the piano, I could listen for hours, as I was swept away to a serene and beautiful landscape of magnificent melodies. Each time Uncle Pat visited, I stuck to him like glue. Uncle Pat didn't have any children of his own. I hoped he would know the love and respect I had for him in naming our first son after him.

David agreed to the arrangement, and we gave our son his father's name for his middle name. Patrick David King. I liked the sound of it. Patrick means *strong*, and David signifies *beloved*, I soon learned. Perfect, I thought, hoping this child would know the Lord's great love for him, and that he would be strong in the Lord all the days of his life.

Normal.

That's the word doctors used over and over to describe my pregnancy. Nothing out of the ordinary. I was in the kitchen talking with a friend when I felt the trickle running down my legs. My water had broken. My friend, who is a nurse, quickly sprung into action, barking out orders to me and hailing her husband on the telephone.

"Go get David King out of that bank board meeting, and tell him his son is on the way!" she said.

David told me they were deep in discussion of loans and profits when someone knocked on the outside door. The elderly gentleman who went to the door shuffled back into the meeting room with a wise grin on his face and said, "Dr. King, it's time!" It was the first occasion a bank board meeting had been interrupted for the birth of a child.

We spent the next 12 hours in and out of contractions, watching the peaks and valleys of my pain on the screen, and listening to the reassuring beeps of Patrick's heartbeat. Finally, at 6:39 a.m., on Friday, March 19, 1993, Patrick came boldly into the world.

That exuberant newborn cry every new mother listens for filled the room.

He's got some good lungs, I thought with amusement.

They placed Patrick on top of my chest and wrapped some warm blankets around the two of us.

"Hello, Patrick. We are so happy you are here," I cooed.

The combined warmth of my words and the cozy heated blanket tripped Patrick's "off" switch, and he stopped crying and immediately nestled into his mother's love. I was hooked. I adored my little boy already.

David brought our daughters to visit the next day. Katie, age six, jumped on the hospital bed where I was holding Patrick.

"Be gentle, honey," her daddy instructed, as Emily, age four, looked out from behind his leg, which she was gripping tightly.
A vivacious redhead with nonstop personality, Katie began telling her brother all about our home and family and the fun they were going to have together. "We are going to be bestest friends, Patrick!" she said.

A shy, deliberate blonde, Emily hung back until her daddy coaxed her into meeting her new brother. She cautiously walked over to the hospital bed and began stroking Patrick's arm. "He is so soft," she whispered. I intuitively knew Emily would be the one to hold, feed, and help take care of Patrick, while Katie would introduce him to all the adventures in life.

Our youngest daughter Sarah was only two years old at the time, and we felt it would be better for her to meet Patrick on familiar ground, at home. The day we brought him home, Sarah, a joyful, curly-haired, blue-eyed blonde, strolled up to Patrick, blanket in hand. When she heard him coo, her eyes grew as large as saucers, and she exclaimed, "It's a bay-bay! That's a bay-bay!" She told everyone in the house who would listen, "It's a bay-bay!" Then, she walked over, held out her blanket, and said, "Do you want my goong, goong?" Her well-loved blanket with the lace trim, her "goong goong" was her prized possession. I knew instantly that she and Patrick were going to get along fine. I thought of Sarah's free spirit and caring nature, and I wondered what sort of personality this new baby would contribute to our family. "Children are a gift from the Lord," says Psalm 127:3, NLT. I couldn't wait to discover what lay inside this precious package . . .

"Something isn't right with Patrick."

I looked at Andrea, the lead teacher in Patrick's two-year-old preschool class.

"It should be time for him to move up to the three-year-old classroom," she said, "but he is not ready."

Not ready! What do you have to be able to do to move from a two-year-old area to a three-year-old area? Alarm crept from my chest to my throat.

Who was I fooling? I knew something wasn't right. Something hadn't been right for a long time. Patrick didn't talk. He was three years old, and not one syllable. Well-meaning people like my mother-in-law kept telling me, "Don't worry. Boys develop more slowly than girls." But instinctively, I knew Patrick was not where he should be developmentally. He wouldn't look anyone in the eyes. He couldn't stand to be touched, arching his back in pain and flailing his arms when he experienced human contact. His favorite pastime was placing a cup on top of a spoon and shaking the spoon so that the cup moved back and forth. He would place that rocking cup directly in front of his face and track it with his eyes for hours. When he didn't have access to his cup and spoon contraption, he would flap his hands in front of his face. Loud noises and strong smells sent him into off-the-charts tantrums. And, if people, even well-meaning children, came into his space and startled him, he often reacted by biting or hitting in an attempt to defend himself and make the painful stimulus go away. This reaction didn't win us any friends at the daycare facility. Then there was the head banging when he got really overwhelmed.

"He's not talking. He doesn't play well with others. He doesn't participate in circle time. He hits and bites. He is always in his own world and doesn't interact with others." Andrea ticked off the long list of reasons why Patrick shouldn't—wouldn't—be moved up to the next age-level classroom.

Dear God, he's failing two-year-old preschool! I thought in shock. *Is that even possible?*

Andrea continued, "There is a Preschool Outreach Program in the county school system. They come out and test children who are considered to be developmentally delayed, and if tests conclude they are behind other students their age, then they begin to work with them right away to try to help them. Would you allow them to test Patrick?"

I was stunned. That was the first time I had heard someone speak the words, "developmentally delayed" in regard to my son.

"Yes! If they could help him, that would be wonderful!" I said.

Little did I know that this would be only the beginning of years of testing.

Patrick's Perspective:

I remember when I hit my head on the floor whenever I got overstimulated. My body felt super tense, and I didn't know what to do. There was a problem, and my body didn't know how to handle it. The head banging was a way to release the tension. I had so much tension in my head, and I felt the only way to release it was to hit my head.

I remember shaking things in front of my face, too. I did that for a long time. It helped me to focus on just one thing when there were lots of things going on around me. Believe it or not, it helped me calm down, too. I got to enter my own world for a while. When I'm seeing things, hearing things, smelling things, getting bumped around, or even when a lot is going on, it's hard for my brain to sort it all out. My brain gets all jumbled up . . . kind of like a traffic jam in New York City.

Even though I still feel tension and get overstimulated today, I have found better ways to deal with those things, like talking to someone, going to a quiet place, listening to music, playing video games, watching a movie, and going on the computer. I feel like I look at things more wisely now, too. In other words, whenever I tense up, I don't have to react in extremes. I can choose to deal with stress in a healthy way.

SOMETHING TO THINK ABOUT:

What is causing you or someone you love to be in agony?

Would you talk with the Lord about it?

What isn't "normal" in your life?

What could you learn from it?

How could you adapt to some of the tensions in your life?

Make a list, and choose one item to incorporate

into your life this week.

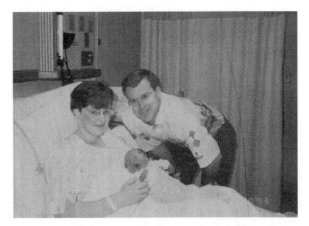

Susan and David with Patrick after his birth

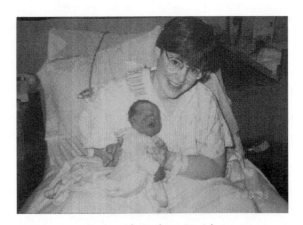

Susan with newborn Patrick

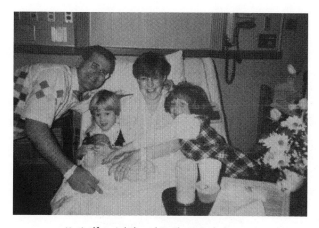

*Katie (far right) and Emily visit their new
baby brother at the hospital*

Sarah welcomes Patrick at home

SUSAN JANE KING

2

A MAZE OF TESTS

"Lord, You are my lamp;
the Lord illuminates my darkness."
—2 Samuel 22:29, HCSB

"**W**e conducted a wide range of tests," said Pat Driver, the preschool outreach coordinator for Rowan County Schools. She went on to recite a long litany of the names of the tests they had administered to Patrick two weeks ago. A kind, soft-spoken woman with cropped gray hair and round glasses, Pat conveyed a sensitive and caring attitude with the information she shared. She carefully discussed every test and each result number.

"The overall result is that although your son is age 3 years and 4 months, his test results put him developmentally at age 1 year and 2 months," Pat said.

I felt like someone had punched me in the stomach. I gasped for breath. *He's not even functioning where he should be for half his age! Why? What's wrong? What haven't I done that I should be doing?*

"What should we do?" I asked Pat, on the verge of tears.

"Well, I would like to start working with him one-on-one to help him try to make some advancement and hopefully get him ready for kindergarten," Pat said. "And I recommend you see your pediatrician and talk with him about having Patrick tested at the Developmental Evaluation Center. They can do a much wider range of tests than we can, and they can recommend and begin some specific therapies to help Patrick with his challenges."

It was the end of the day, and I walked out of Patrick's daycare, The Rowan Medical Child Development Center, in a daze. As I made my way to the car, I realized I was beginning to tread down a path I had never been on before.

God, please help me! I cried.

Patrick plodded alongside me into the one-story brick building with the words "Concord Developmental Evaluation Center" on the front. I was thrilled that Patrick was cooperating at this point, going with me into what would surely be a maze of unsettling sights, sounds, smells, and stimuli. One little trigger could send him off into the throes of fits and screaming. That would be the point of no return.

Lord, please help us get some answers today. Please help Patrick stay calm. Please let the test administrators be kind and sensitive toward him, I silently prayed.

We were told that we would be at the DEC most of the day, from 8 a.m. to around 2 or 3 p.m. I had packed a lunch for Patrick, with the same things he always ate every day for lunch: a peanut butter and jelly sandwich with the crusts cut off, apples with the skin cut off, and pretzels. I had tucked a juice box into the collection of food as an extra treat.

Patrick required—no, demanded—sameness in his world. He settled into predictability like a cat soaking up the sun in the kitchen window. Predictability meant not mixing the textures of food. No gelatin with fruit mixed in, or cookies with nuts. It was too difficult for him to sort out the different sensory impressions. When we drove to church, we had to take the same route every time. God help us if we had to take a detour! The unfamiliar images would send Patrick reeling down into that dark pit of uncertainty, scratching and clawing to find a way out.

At the DEC, Patrick had social work, medical, psychological, educational, speech and language, occupational therapy, and hearing assessments. He was administered the following tests:

* Stanford Binet Intelligence Scale

* Leiter International Performance Scale

* Vineland Adaptive Behavior Scale

* Childhood Autism Rating Scale

* Kaufman Survey of Early Academic and Language Skills

* Preschool Language Scale

* Reynell Developmental Language Scales

* Rossetti Infant-Toddler Language Scale

* Receptive One Word Picture Vocabulary Test

* Expressive One Word Picture Vocabulary Test

They analyzed his oral motor skills, voice, fluency, and articulation, and they examined his hearing abilities. Patrick cooperated through the long series of tests, although he seemed dazed and confused through several of them. By the end of the day, with his nervous system taxed to the limit, his glazed eyes and weak shuffle made him look like a zombie as he left the last testing room.

This was just the beginning of the many tests we endured over the years. We had more in-depth hearing tests. *Maybe he wasn't talking because he couldn't hear.* Wrong. The results were normal.

We also had a sleep-deprived EEG or electroencephalogram. That was an adventure! I had to keep him awake all night long, and then take him to the testing center, where he immediately fell asleep and they measured his brain wave activity. Praise the Lord for the 24-hour Walmart! I put him in a cart and walked the aisles. We had been there before, and Patrick was familiar with the long rows of brightly colored objects. He studied every one of them all night long. I thought to myself, *I bet if he could talk, he would give them an inventory of this entire store!*

Patrick plunged into a deep sleep the moment I laid him on the testing bed at 9 a.m. Afterward, the doctor sat me down and told me Patrick's brain waves were slower on the right side of his brain, which was not normal. He added that this particular part of the brain sorts out input from all of Patrick's different senses. No wonder Patrick bolted into sensory overload so easily!

"What should we do?" I asked.

The doctor looked down at my son and said, "There's nothing you can do about that."

The tests at the DEC were extensive and confusing. I felt drained, exhausted. I entered every session with a mixture of fear and hope. Fear that we might receive more bad news or that something would trigger an explosive reaction from Patrick. Hope that we might finally get some answers, and more importantly, some help for my son.

I felt like I was stumbling around in a completely dark cave, trying to find my way. An occasional unknown rock along the path would send me sprawling forward, and I would have to right myself again and keep going. But through it all, I knew the Lord was there. Even if I didn't know the way, He did. "If I say, 'Surely the darkness will overwhelm me, and the light around me will be night,' even the darkness is not dark to You [Lord], and the night is as bright as the day. Darkness and light are alike to You" (Psalm 139:11-12, NASB). I knew the Lord would lead me through these myriad tests. I depended on Him, at the gut-level. Nothing else could—or would—be able to lead me into the light.

The social worker from the Developmental Evaluation Center thumbed through the half-inch thick report in her lap. I wished I could snatch the stack of papers out of her hand and escape to a secluded corner somewhere to read them.

"Patrick is extremely delayed developmentally," she said, keeping her focus on the pages. "He did much better in testing that did not involve language of any kind. He does not understand language at all. His diagnosis at this point is pervasive developmental disorder." She looked up, gazing into my eyes. "That means, across the board, he is way behind other children his age."

She continued, looking back down at her notes, "He also has sensory integration dysfunction, which means that when he gets input from all his senses, that input is not processed well and causes him pain and discomfort as his brain tries to sort it all out." I already knew the things she was telling me. I just didn't know the medical names for the conditions that plagued my little boy.

"And, based on all our findings, your son can be classified as having mental retardation," she added in a crisp, definitive voice. What? My mind exploded in a million pieces. I couldn't think straight.

The social worker continued, unaware of the shattered thoughts and feelings that lay strewn all over the floor of my heart. I could feel the tears beginning to sting my eyes.

"And we think your son might have autism," she added, which dealt the final blow to any strength I had remaining, physically or emotionally. I could feel my legs and arms start to tremble.

Autism. Those are the people who sit and rock in corners all day. Autism?

The social worker went on, "We aren't qualified to make a diagnosis of autism, however, so you will need to fill out this paperwork and submit it to the TEACCH Center in Charlotte, where they can assess your son and make a more accurate diagnosis."

She put a stack of papers into my hands. Then, she handed me the DEC Evaluation.

Wanting to end on a positive note, she said, "The good news is that we can start working with your son immediately. We recommend occupational therapy twice a week to help him with his sensory integration issues. And we can refer you to a speech therapist, who can try to help your son with his language issues. You should see the speech therapist twice a week, too. There also is an excellent program at the University of North Carolina at Charlotte where they will work with your son twice a week to improve his perceptual motor development. Here is a brochure on that program," she said, adding it to the papers stacked in my lap.

As I left the DEC, a cold February wind blew right through me. I couldn't feel anything, except a growing emptiness inside of me. Where was the little boy who was going to play catch with his daddy and build forts in the woods? Would he even be able to say "Daddy" someday?

Lord, help me! I prayed. *I know You say You will never leave us or forsake us* (Hebrews 13:5, NIV). *I believe that. HELP ME to believe that!*

Patrick's Perspective:

Routines and having things a certain way help me and other autistic people. For a while, we always had to drive to church the same way. My schedule during the day had to be the same. My lunch always had to be the same. I would even line up my videotapes in the same line all the time. The sameness meant that there were less things to sort out and try to understand. I have gotten better over the years at handling unexpected things. God has helped me with this. I don't remember much about all the tests I had when I was younger. I remember going to some of the therapy places. I am grateful to have gotten the help that I needed. They helped me develop the abilities that I needed for the future. I agree with the Bible verse that says even in the dark times, God can help us (Psalm 139:11-12, NASB).

SOMETHING TO THINK ABOUT:

What might you be experiencing today that

might be preparing you for the future?

Is there something in your life that you

feel powerless against?

Think about some of your challenges and limitations.

Would you acknowledge that God has the

final say about those things?

Where do you need answers in your life?

Would you ask the Lord to lead you into the truth?

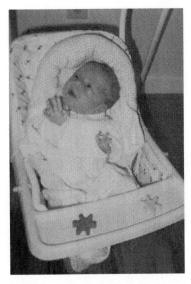

*Sounds, smells, movements, and touch
startled Patrick from a young age*

*Infant Patrick
(Photo by Karen Goforth)*

Patrick at 15 months
(Photo by Karen Goforth)

Patrick, age 3
(Photo by Karen Goforth)

SUSAN JANE KING

3

"YOUR SON HAS AUTISM"

"'For I know the plans I have for you,' declares the Lord,
'plans to prosper you and not to harm you,
plans to give you hope and a future.'"
—Jeremiah 29:11, NIV

I stared at the huge stack of papers looming like a mountain before me. The TEACCH Center paperwork asked for so many details about Patrick—my pregnancy, his birth, developmental stages, mannerisms, as well as my impressions as his mother. How could I put into words all the details about this precious son of mine? How could I get them to understand who he is and how he processes the world around him?

Ever efficient and strong, my husband David had completed his stack of forms with concise one or two-word answers. My answers consisted of lengthy sentences and explanations. *I have to get this right. I don't want to leave anything out,* I thought desperately, as if my answers would provide the solution to Patrick's issues. *I've got to get this done.* Panic set in. *I know there is an 18-month wait after the paperwork is received. Get it done, Susan!*

At the time, the TEACCH Center was voted the best program in the United States by the National Institute of Health for people with autism and their families. Developed at the University of North Carolina at Chapel Hill, the program's focus is to assess, train, and educate people who have autism and to assist their families, with an aim to help them be as successful as possible in navigating the world.

When I started looking into the TEACCH Center, I was told that people in the military who had autistic children often requested to be based in North Carolina so that they could receive TEACCH services, which were free to North Carolina residents at that time. *Lord, I am so thankful You had us move to North Carolina six years before Patrick was born. Look at how You provided for us! I am so grateful. Give me the wisdom to know what to put on these forms. I trust You with the results.*

On October 29, 1998, David and I sat in a circle of chairs with a group of professionals from the TEACCH Center: Sue McCarter, a psychoeducational therapist and parent consultant; Lori Brandon, PhD, a parent consultant and licensed practicing psychologist; and David Crnobori, a client therapist. They had reviewed our forms and had assessed Patrick's development during several of his visits to the center.

"We reviewed our test results and your comments," Sue said. "Based on all the information, we have given your son a diagnosis of mild autism."

She stopped, giving us time to process her words. One of the other specialists in the room softly asked, "How are you feeling in light of that information?"

David spoke up first, and I was glad. My mind was swimming with this new piece of information. "We're okay. It's nice to know what it is after all these years." Patrick was 5. "Now that we know what it is, we can start helping him more."

I just kept nodding. It sounded good. But inside me, something was building, a huge and heavy force that I couldn't explain. I tried to keep my eyes bright and my mouth plastered with a smile.

"Wonderful," the specialist said. "We would like to suggest a few preliminary meetings with our staff, where we can develop a treatment plan tailored to Patrick's specific needs. We can adjust the plan as we go along. We would like you to bring Patrick to our offices once a week after that. During that time, we will work on implementing that plan and on checking to see how Patrick and your family are doing in this new world of autism."

New world of autism.

I felt like I had gotten off a train at the wrong stop. This was not the destination I had expected when we began Patrick's testing. How were we going to adapt in this new place we knew nothing about? How was he going to live in this world the rest of his life?

They handed me some information about autism and their center.

According to the Centers for Disease Control, about one in every 68 children has been identified with an autism spectrum disorder. The CDC Web site states,

> Autism spectrum disorders (ASDs) are a group of developmental disabilities that can cause significant social, communication and behavioral challenges. People with ASDs handle information in their brain differently than other people. ASDs are spectrum disorders. That means ASDs affect each person in different ways, and can range from very mild to severe. People with autistic disorder usually have significant language delays, social and communication challenges, and unusual behaviors and interests. Many people with autistic disorder also have intellectual disability.[i]

The folks at the TEACCH Center handed me a brochure from the Autism Society of North Carolina. I scanned its definition of autism and hesitated over the words, "no known cure."

The brochure told me we were entering a completely new and unfamiliar world, and we would be stuck there—forever.

David and I walked back to our van in silence. I thought I had prepared myself for this possibility. I thought I was ready to hear the "A" word. But whatever started building in that little circle of chairs erupted the minute I sat in the van. I started sobbing uncontrollably.

David quickly moved into protective mode. "It's going to be okay," he said. "It's going to be okay." I saw his jaw tighten and his shoulders square as he said, "We are going to do everything we can to help Patrick. There have been people with autism who have gone on to be college professors. We don't know what the future holds. We are going to be optimistic."

I looked over at David, so grateful to have married a strong, wise man. But, at the same time, I felt myself descending into a bottomless pit. And I wasn't even trying to grab onto anything, to find my way out. I was just sinking deeper and deeper into the unknown.

In a sense, I had just experienced a death—the demise of my dreams and expectations for my child. Like anyone experiencing a death, I had to go through the grieving process. Experts claim there are five steps to the grieving process: denial, anger, bargaining, depression, and acceptance.[ii] I bypassed the first three and hit step four with a loud thud.

Vibrant drumbeats, pulsating rhythms, and bounding melodies played about in the distant recesses of my hearing. Praise music filled the air at the Women of Faith Conference in Charlotte, North Carolina. *Lord, I don't want to be here. Lord, I HATE being here!* Less than 24 hours before, David and I had been told that our son had autism. Now, I was surrounded by thousands of excited, joyful women who were praising the Lord, singing songs of worship, and listening to Bible teachers. I had agreed months before to go with a group of girlfriends from China Grove. We had even reserved a hotel room in the "big city" as sort of a girls' retreat weekend. But that was before . . . before my life had turned upside down. Now, I just wanted to crawl under a rock somewhere and die.

"You should go," David had urged. "It will be good for you. You have been looking forward to this. It would be good to take your mind off Patrick for a little while and think about something else, to be with someone else." He eventually convinced me, mainly because I didn't have the energy to put up a fight. Now, I was regretting my decision.

My friends didn't know. I didn't have the strength to tell them. I was afraid the dam would break, and I would collapse in a flood of tears. It was all still too raw. Too painful. So I put on a smile and moved along with the flow of thousands walking the arena.

The first several speakers didn't capture my attention. "It would be good to take your mind off Patrick for a little while," David had said. I couldn't. He was always on my mind.

Then Marilyn Meberg got up to speak. She started sharing about her daughter Joanie, who was born with spina bifida.

"Joanie lived 15 months and then died," Marilyn said.

Her words ripped open the thick veil hanging over me. My eyes and ears were drawn to her words.

"At first, I was really angry with God," she said. "I didn't understand why He let this happen to me. I loved Him. I served Him. I had Bible study in my house, and people came to know Jesus at that Bible study.

"For months, I just wore a mask," she said, "pretending everything was okay. Continuing along with my life. Not talking to God or anyone about how I was feeling."

That's exactly what I was doing. Everything stood still as I was drawn into her message.

"Then, one day, the Lord told me, 'You don't have to wear a mask with Me. It's okay to tell Me you are disappointed,'" Marilyn said.

With those words, all the walls I had built up around myself came crumbling down, and I started crying.

Okay, Lord. I'm disappointed. This is not how it was supposed to go. What about Patrick? Life is going to be so hard for him. And I don't feel equipped to raise an autistic child. I CAN'T DO IT!

"You're right," I heard the Lord's gentle, loving voice whisper to my heart. "You can't. But we can. Will you trust Me?"

I caught my breath, as all of time froze in that instant. And I knew why I was living in such a dark place.

I wasn't trusting the Lord.

That's why I had descended into that dark pit. I had stopped looking at Him, listening to Him, clinging to Him, relying on Him.
"Lean on, trust in, and be confident in the Lord with all your heart and mind, and do not rely on your own insight or understanding. In all your ways know, recognize, and acknowledge Him, and He will direct and make straight and plain your paths" (Proverbs 3:5-6, Amp).

Okay, I responded feebly. *Yes*, I said with more conviction. *I will trust You!*

This diagnosis of autism was not a surprise to the Lord. He knew it was coming. He had a purpose in it. He had a reason for making Patrick autistic. God doesn't do random.

My feet hit the bottom of that pit and bounced off it as if they had hit a spring-loaded trampoline. I was out!

Patrick's Perspective:

Proverbs 3:5-6 is one of my favorite Bible verses. It says to trust in God with all my heart and not to lean on my own understanding; in all my ways, to acknowledge God, and He will direct my steps.

It can be really stressful being autistic. But I know I can go to God, and He will help me. That's what I do every day. I ask Him to help me. I ask Him to show me what He wants me to do. And He does.

I am so happy that He is always with me and that I am never alone when I am with Him. Life is great when God is in charge.

Like my mom, I don't always know what's ahead of me in life and how I am going to handle things, so I just have to choose to trust God, knowing that He will lead me down the path that is best for me and for Him.

I also like reading my Bible. I know that everything God says is true. That's part of trusting Him and not leaning on my own understanding. I just know God says it, so it's true. I choose to believe it.

The Bible also says, "Trust in Him at all times, O people; pour out your heart before Him; God is a refuge for us" (Psalm

62:8, NASB). I know when I am having a hard time that I can tell God how I am feeling, and He will help me to trust Him, just like He did for my mom.

SOMETHING TO THINK ABOUT:

What are you disappointed about?

What fears are you facing about the future?

Would you choose to trust God at this very moment,

knowing that He holds you and your future in His hands?

Would you trust Him to lead the way?

Talk to God about your concerns, and conclude by

personalizing Proverbs 3:5-6 to your life:

Lord, I am going to trust in You with all my heart. I don't have this figured out, but I don't have to understand everything—because You do. In all the things I do, I am going to acknowledge You as God, my God. I know You love and take care of me, and You will direct my steps. Thank you for holding my future in Your hands.

Patrick around the age of his diagnosis

4

TALKING

"By my God I can leap over a wall."
—*2 Samuel 22:30, NASB*

"**W**hat are your greatest concerns regarding Patrick?" Sue McCarter asked, pen and clipboard in hand. I had come to love and respect this kind and strong advocate for people with autism and their families. Her voice conveyed a strength and reassurance.

"Well, he doesn't talk," I replied. "I can tell he wants to communicate, but he doesn't know how to. He doesn't understand language, and he gets very frustrated. And we get frustrated, too. I just want to help him."

"That is a common problem with autism," Sue said. "We will set that as our first goal for Patrick, to create some form of communication system for him." She continued writing notes on her clipboard and adjusted her glasses.

"What else?" she asked.

"Well, I can't get him to do things," I said. "I don't know if it's because he can't understand me or what, but for example, if he has papers to do for school, or practice work for the speech therapist or occupational therapist, he doesn't understand what he is supposed to do or how to organize himself."

"Okay. We'll put down a goal of providing structure for accomplishing tasks," Sue added, as her pencil scratched more details onto her papers.

"And one more thing," I added, hesistant. "Can I add

another thing?"

"Of course!" Sue smiled.

"This one isn't so much about Patrick, himself, but it's a real problem," I said. "My daughters don't understand about Patrick. We have tried to explain autism to them, but they don't get it. All they can see is that Patrick gets treated differently than them. They think he gets away with things, and they even think we love him more because he gets so much of our time and attention and because we don't discipline him the way we discipline them. One of them even calls him, 'the prince.'"

"How old are your daughters?" Sue asked.

"Ages 7, 9, and 11," I said. "I don't think they know how to handle him either. They come running and screaming into the room where Patrick is, all excited about something, and one of them will grab Patrick and hug him, all out of love, and he goes crazy, screaming noises, throwing out his arms, and kicking. It's because they have entered his space unexpectedly, and he can't sort out all of those sudden sensory invasions. I've tried to explain to the girls that they can't do that, but they don't understand why."

"So let's put as our third goal to help Patrick's siblings understand about his autism and relate to him in an appropriate way," Sue said.

"That would be wonderful," I said, relieved that reinforcements were on the way.

"I'm going to have our team put some thought into these goals and develop some strategies for each one of them," Sue said. "And then we'll get back together next week. Is that okay?"

"That is fantastic," I said, realizing that the heavy load I had been carrying in trying to help my son and our family was now also being shouldered by our new friends at the TEACCH Center. *Lord, thank You for this help—Your help*, I prayed.

"Have you ever used pictures to communicate with Patrick?" Sue asked, as we addressed our main goal at a later date.

"No," I said. "I never thought of it."

"Well, most autistic people are very visually oriented. They really see things. So even though they may not understand words they hear, they often can understand pictures they see," Sue said.

I straightened up in my chair. We were blazing a new trail here—one so different from the dark path of the diagnosis. I was excited to discover what lay ahead of us.

"The pictures can help Patrick make sense of his world," Sue said. She pulled out a blue folder and opened it to reveal a white strip of fuzzy Velcro pasted down the center vertically. "This is a very useful tool for our clients. You can stick pictures along this Velcro strip to communicate with Patrick . . .what is happening, what you want him to do, what he is about to experience, how you feel . . . and he hopefully will understand through the pictures."

"What kind of pictures?" I asked.

"Well, they're more like cartoon caricatures," Sue said. She brought out a clear plastic bag filled with 2-inch by 2-inch picture squares that had small pieces of Velcro on the back. "Here, for example, is a picture of a toothbrush." I looked at the artwork of the bright red toothbrush with white shiny bristles. "That lets Patrick know it is time to brush his teeth," Sue said. "Here is a picture of a bed." I gazed at the full-sized bed with the inviting plump blue comforter and the downy, soft pillows. "That lets Patrick know it is time to go to bed. And if you line up the pictures like this," Sue continued, pasting the toothbrush at the top of the folder and the bed directly below it, "then Patrick knows he needs to brush his teeth and after that go to bed."

"There are all kinds of pictures in this packet," Sue said. "And you can make your own pictures to address things specific to Patrick's lifestyle."

Hope began to take hold in my heart. *Would I be able to communicate with my son?* The possibility loomed like the potential of a bright sunrise on the horizon of my soul, and the earliest rays of dawn had started to peek through the darkness.

I held out the blue Velcro-lined folder with the picture of our family van in the center of it. I made sure it slowly moved into the center of Patrick's gaze. His eyes caught the colors and began to study them. Recognition. I could see it rise to the surface and illuminate his eyes. He stood up from the floor and walked to the back door, where he turned expectantly and waited.

He knows! Dear Jesus, he knows!

I walked over and opened the door. He lifted up his hand and took mine, and I carefully served as his counter-weight as he methodically placed each foot on the multitude of steps leading to the garage floor. He walked over to the sliding door of our family van and looked up at me again with the same expectant look.

I opened the door.

With my help, he stepped up and in, climbing into his car seat. Another expectant look.

I buckled the straps in place, my fingers trembling.

He was in. He wasn't screaming.

I dug into the picture bag and placed three more pictures on the Velcro strip: a piano, a house, and a television. I showed them to Patrick. His eyes went up and down the pictures, unlocking new mysteries for him. He looked at me again.

He knew.

The girls piled into the car with their piano books, laughing and giggling, being ever careful not to bump or prod their brother. We drove to their piano lessons, and after I carefully deposited them at Mrs. Carter's house, Patrick and I drove back to our home, where he went back inside and finished watching his television program.

No tantrums. No kicking and shrieking.

The pictures were a map, telling Patrick about the territory ahead, and he was learning to understand that map very quickly.

"House," I would say each time I pointed to the caricature. "Van." "Brush teeth." "Clothes." My hope was that someday, the sounds would mean something, too.

Patrick made sounds, but they made no sense. He would come up to me and cup my face in his little hands and make noises, trying to communicate. I wanted so desperately to understand him, to give him what he needed. Oftentimes, we both would end up in a crumpled heap on the floor, frustrated by the desire to understand and be understood, and not being able to do either.

I loved reading books to my children, and Patrick would sit with me, studying the bright-colored pictures and listening to the rising and falling rhythm of my voice. Most of the books were the typical childhood fairy tales, and many of them ended with, "And they all lived happily ever after."

One day, after I had finished reading him one of the books and had closed its cover, Patrick looked off into the distance and said, "And they all lived happily ever after."

I froze. He had just spoken! And not just one word but a whole string of words.

"Patrick?" I said with delight and apprehension.

Was it too good to be true? Was he really speaking?

He pushed himself off the couch and began walking around the house, repeating over and over, "And they all lived happily ever after."

"He's not really *speaking*," the doctor told me sympathetically.

I had just gushed about Patrick's 7-word wonder sentence.

"What Patrick is doing is called echolalia," the doctor said. "He hears the words. He likes the sound of them, but he has no idea what they mean. He has simply learned to repeat the noises he hears. It is not speech as far as communication is concerned."

I sat there deflated, letting the truth of what he had said sink in. Patrick could make sounds now that imitated words, but he didn't understand what they meant.

I had jumped up and down the first time he had said, "And they all lived happily ever after," celebrating the fact that he could talk. I still celebrated it. It was something new. A glimmer of hope. But now, that phrase rolled off his tongue all day long, over and over. "And they all lived happily ever after. And they all lived happily ever after. And they all lived happily ever after." That early delight was giving rise to annoyance.

Would there be a happily ever after for him? For us? Oh, how I longed for it.

"House," I said, pointing to the picture.

"House," Patrick repeated.

For a long time, Patrick had been repeating the sounds of the words associated with the pictures.

"Van," I said.

"Van," he repeated.

He had become an expert at repeating the sounds of words. His favorite sound string was still, "And they all lived happily ever after," but he was adding new sounds to his symphony of life.

"Piano," I said.

"Piano," he parroted.

Lord, please help these sounds to mean something to him. Please open up the world of words to him, I prayed.

"House."

"House."

"TV."

"TV."

Then, he stopped.

He ran his fingers down the strip of pictures neatly lining his blue Velcro folder. He looked at me with a steady gaze, and he said, "Okay. We are going to get in the van and take the girls to their piano lesson. Then we are going to come back home, and I can watch TV . . . Okay."

That wasn't a repetition of sounds. That was *thinking* expressed in words, words with meaning!

I wanted to scream, to jump up and down. But I knew that kind of behavior would throw Patrick into a full-blown fit. I tried to catch my breath while I rejoiced in the depths of my soul.

Patrick was talking, *really* talking. He had entered the world of words.

"Nothing is impossible with God" (Luke 1:37, NLT). Doctors told us Patrick might not ever talk, yet he did. The Lord always has the final say—about everything. I learned that as Patrick blazed a trail into the realm of words.

Patrick's Perspective:

When I was younger, I knew what objects were in my head. I just did not know how to express what they were. The pictures helped a lot. I remember my blue Velcro folder. It went to school with me, and to my Sunday School class at church. I liked seeing the pictures to know what was going to happen or what people wanted me to do.

This system helped solve lots of problems because before the pictures, I didn't understand why I was being moved around or what was going to happen to me, and I would get upset. When I came to church, I remember my teachers would line up the pictures for me in Sunday School to tell me what we were going to do, and they would give me tokens when I would complete each task. They helped make my world more predictable and less scary.

I am a very visual person. That is a challenge and a blessing. I can remember things when I see them. I see pictures in my mind. That can help when memorizing visual things for school, like the Periodic Table of the Elements, or creating visual ideas in my brain. But things that aren't visual—things you have to infer—they are harder for me to understand.

I remember that I enjoyed reading the Dr. Seuss books.

They were colorful and creative, and they were full of interesting word sounds. I still make up words because they sound cool to me.

I am literal about stuff. Most autistic people have this trait. It means that when you tell us something, we take whatever you say as fact. For example, when I was about 8 years old, a nice lady at church told me I was so cute she wanted to eat me up. I went screaming down the hall because I thought she was really going to do that.

Communication is a problem for most autistic people. We often don't understand what people actually mean. And we do not know how to talk to people a lot of the time. We want to communicate, but it is confusing. When I was in elementary and middle school, I did not know how to talk with people and how to enter conversations. I joined conversations the wrong way, and I talked too long about my interests. I would interrupt people's conversations by inserting comments about something unrelated to the conversation. Over the years, I have figured out more of the rules about how to talk with other people.

Today, it still can be a challenge to communicate because I cannot always interpret people's facial expressions. But I enjoy talking with friends and keeping up with their lives. I am grateful that I can understand language and the communication process.

SOMETHING TO THINK ABOUT:

What limitations has the Lord helped you to overcome?

What walls do you see in your life today?

Would you give your limitations to the Lord

and look to Him for help?

*Patrick delighted in the pictures and
sounds associated with books
(Photo by Karen Goforth)*

*A thoughtful Patrick . . . around the age
where he began to truly talk
(Photo by Karen Goforth)*

5

ORGANIZING THE WORLD

*"There is a time for everything,
and a season for every activity under the heavens."*
—Ecclesiastes 3:1, NIV

Even though Patrick was communicating and understanding words, we still used his blue Velcro folder with the picture strips. David jokingly said that Patrick was the only 6-year-old he knew who had a daily planner!

The picture folder went to school with Patrick, where teachers would line up the photos to explain the class schedule or to ask Patrick to perform a task. Even his Sunday School teachers embraced the picture folder. They would line up the Bible, crayons, and scissors on the Velcro strip, and Patrick would know there would be a Bible story, then he would color something, and then cut out the picture. I grew ever more grateful for the countless teachers, professionals, and friends who poured their love, encouragement, and energy into helping my son better understand the confusing world around him.

The pictures continued to help Patrick make sense of the world, what was going to happen, what was expected of him. Words came at him too fast. He often had trouble sorting out the meanings of words strung together so closely and quickly. The blue folder went everywhere with us. I spent hours on the computer finding clip art and creating picture squares relevant to Patrick's routine and life in the King house: clothes (for "get dressed"), two folded hands (for "say prayers"), pill tablets (for "take your medicine"), a mouth (for "do speech therapy"), a toothbrush (for "brush your teeth").

Ugh! Brush your teeth. Patrick hated that ritual. He didn't like the sensory impressions of the brush with its pokey bristles in his mouth, and he hated the taste of mint toothpaste. I scoured the shelves in many different stores until I found a children's watermelon-flavored toothpaste. Even then, I had to start with a dab of the paste on a cotton washcloth and gradually get Patrick to accept having his teeth touched and cleaned before I set out to conquer the introduction of a real toothbrush. It took weeks of practice and patience while Patrick arched his back, gagged, spit, and finally learned to accept this bristly intruder.

Tastes and textures often loomed as enormous giants before Patrick. They threatened him. They created impressions and sensations he often could not interpret. They made him feel strange. Getting him to try and accept new experiences or uncomfortable feelings presented a tremendous challenge. That's why we were so grateful for an angel named Anjoli. *Her name almost looks like the word Angel,* I thought when we first met her.

We had taken a long road to get there. After completing what seemed like endless stacks of paperwork to be accepted for occupational therapy at a place called Amos Cottage in Winston-Salem, I had received a call at work, telling me that they had made a mistake. Patrick was not in their service area. I would have to apply to the Concord Developmental Evaluation Center instead. I closed the door to my office and cried. I was sure we were supposed to go to Amos Cottage. Everyone had said such wonderful things about it.

I learned something significant from that experience. We might have plans about how we think things should go, but God always has the best plans. Scripture says, "The mind of man plans his way, but the Lord directs his steps" (Proverbs 16:9, NASB).

As time passed, I was extremely grateful that the Lord had redirected our steps. When we finally got to the Concord DEC for occupational therapy, Patrick and I were greeted by Anjoli Soman, a warm, endearing woman from India, with a strong spirit and tender heart. She coaxed, cajoled, commanded, and comforted

Patrick into pushing his senses to the limit for an entire hour twice each week. She would push his fingers into thick, goopy mixtures. She would make him smell strong syrups. She would roll him on bolsters, twirl him on swings, apply pressures on his arms and legs, and expose him to a cacophony of sounds. And she miraculously could convince him to try to tie his shoes, button buttons, cut with scissors, hop, skip, and jump. Every one of Patrick's feeble attempts was rewarded with praise and sometimes stickers. (Patrick was still in love with pictures.)

Anjoli coached me, too. One therapy to continue at home involved brushing Patrick with a soft, nylon-bristled "sensory brush" three times each day on his back, arms, and legs.

"The brush sends lots of impulses along Patrick's nerves to his brain," Anjoli said. "Sensory impressions to his brain get tangled together as his brain tries to process them. All these many impulses at once from the brushing help break up the tangles."

I imagined a giant explosive being detonated on the logjam in Patrick's brain. It helped me remain faithful in the brushing routine.

"It is extremely important for children like Patrick to get help as soon as possible," Anjoli said. "At a certain point in development, the nerve pathways in the brain sort of 'finalize' themselves, and it's more difficult to make progress."

Those words drove me to take Patrick to his multitude of therapies every week. Our family calendar looked like a balloon that was about to pop. It was filled to the bursting point.

But, little by little, the many therapies helped Patrick to better process the world around him. He gradually made some improvements in tolerating the daily barrage of sights, sounds, smells, and touches that invaded his world.

And he discovered the delightful world of shoeboxes.

"We have a shoebox system for helping autistic individuals organize their lives and the tasks required of them," Sue McCarter said.

"Shoeboxes?" I asked.

"Yes," she said. "We use shoeboxes, or the plastic containers with a lid that are about the size of shoeboxes. You can find them in a lot of different stores.

"You create a shoebox for each task you want Patrick to complete. For example, if he is supposed to complete a math paper for homework and color the picture at the top of the page, you would put the paper, a pencil, and crayons in the box with the lid on it. If he is supposed to practice cutting out pictures for occupational therapy, you would put the paper with the pictures on it inside another box with a pair of scissors. You would number the boxes on the outside, with '1, 2, 3,' etc. Patrick would work with one box at a time, putting his completed work inside and securing the lid in place once he is done. We have found this system helps our clients compartmentalize their world, literally boxing in the demands of their environment into manageable tasks."

The shoeboxes helped Patrick navigate through life's many stresses and strains, requests, and requirements. He could actually "see" some of his responsibilities for the day, and he felt proud each time he could snap the lid on top of a completed box.

Whenever Patrick is about to experience something new, I try to prepare him ahead of time, by telling him what to expect . . . what he might see, hear, and smell. And I try to explain the "social rules" for different situations—what he should and should not do in that setting. That seems to help him.

Also, every person with autism usually has an area of unique strength or interest. It helps in the midst of all their struggles to receive encouragement in those areas. For example, Patrick is very interested in video games and wants to be a video game designer one day. We subscribe to video game magazines for him. We play and talk about video games with him. And we ask him about and listen to his ideas for the games he wants to invent—which are fascinating, by the way.

Order and structure are part of the world God created. I can see it all around me. Like Patrick, I feel much more relaxed when I cooperate with the Lord in bringing order into my life. "For God is not the author of confusion, but of peace" (1 Corinthians 14:33, KJV). I have found He will set the elements of my life in order if I will allow Him to do that, if I permit Him to set up the shoeboxes. He has times and seasons and structures for everything, and they are beautiful.

Patrick's Perspective:

Working with Anjoli definitely stressed my nervous system. Sometimes, I would hide under the bench in the lobby because I knew what was coming. Anjoli had to coax me out from under that bench many times, and I am glad she did! The occupational therapy helped me.

I remember the "trauma" of learning to brush my teeth. I used that watermelon toothpaste until I went to college. I did not want to be seen with a kid's toothpaste in the boys' bathroom, so I made myself get used to mint toothpaste. I also remember fanning out my lunch box and putting my head inside it during kindergarten lunchtime to avoid the jarring smells from the kids I called "the tray people." Sometimes, I would pull my shirt up over my nose to screen out strong smells. I did that all the way through middle school.

Loud sounds bothered me. I hear things louder than other people do. For example, I can hear the electricity humming inside wall outlets. They would always have to warn me at school if they were going to have a fire alarm drill and set off the fire alarm. I would put my hands over my ears when sounds got too loud. I still do that. I definitely had to do that when I rode in the limousine for prom and the driver played this super loud rock music the whole way there!

I ran out screaming from a lot of my occupational therapy sessions. But today, I am grateful for them. I could not tie my shoes until I was 13, but I did learn to tie them! I could not cut with a scissors or write with a pencil, but now I can. I even learned to drive a car after lots and lots of practice. Driving was a challenge because it required using a lot of different senses at once. I think the occupational therapy helped me develop skills for later tasks like driving.

I do not remember the shoeboxes too well. But I have always liked having structure and organization. Today, I have a planner that contains all my appointments, school assignments, and activities. I like the way it keeps me organized and helps me meet my responsibilities. In college, I use my cellphone to check my email and stay in touch with people. Technology today can truly benefit autistic people.

SOMETHING TO THINK ABOUT:

Where do you need to establish some

order or organization in your life?

Would you commit your schedule and responsibilities to

the Lord and ask Him to bring order into your life?

Have you ever been required to do something

beneficial that made you uncomfortable?

Can you look back and see how the Lord

strengthened and helped you?

Would you rely on Him today to do the same?

*School-age Patrick, who learned to use
shoeboxes to organize himself*

6

WALKING IN PATRICK'S SHOES

"Be sympathetic, love one another,
be compassionate and humble."
—1 Peter 3:8, NIV

My heart went out to my daughters. They were young and needed attention, too. They didn't understand about Patrick's autism. My saying, "His brain works differently than yours," wasn't cutting it with them. Praise God for the TEACCH Center!

"Bring in the girls, and we will explain to them about Patrick's autism," Sue said.

So, one crisp autumn afternoon, I loaded up the three girls and Patrick into our family van and headed to the TEACCH Center. *Oh Lord, please help them understand their brother. Help them appreciate him for who he is*, I prayed.

I didn't want them growing up to resent Patrick or the time I had to spend with him to help him. I knew God gave us Patrick for special reasons, many of which were still unfolding. I wanted them to learn to trust God in the midst of everything, which I was still learning to do.

"Why don't you stay out here in the lobby with Patrick while we take the girls back and talk with them?" Sue said.

"Okay," I said. "Have fun girls!" I hoped the positive tone of my voice would wash over them and take hold.

In an hour or so, Katie came bounding back into the room,

her auburn hair flowing behind her like the jet stream of an airplane. I could tell her flight pattern was in direct line with her brother, who was standing on the other side of the room, his eyes trained on the multiple colors and patterns found in a painting on the lobby wall. My autism alert system immediately went into effect.

I struggled to intercept Katie before she initiated a major meltdown. Emily and Sarah were trailing along behind Katie. Their pace was much slower and contemplative, their eyes full of wonder. I instinctively knew I would not reach Katie before she bombarded her brother with a barrage of unexpected sensory input. I braced myself for the chain reaction. Suddenly, Katie jerked herself to a halt. Her brother, aware of his sister's presence, steadily turned his gaze toward her.

"May I give you a hug?" Katie asked.

I caught my breath.

She had never asked for permission before.

Patrick slowly nodded, and Katie gently put her arms around him and squeezed. Emily and Sarah had reached them by now, and they, too, asked for permission to embrace their brother. Patrick agreed, and I watched a miracle unfold before my eyes as my four children held on to each other and freely gave and received one another's love. Patrick had prepared his nervous system for that encounter because he knew it was coming. A new light had dawned for my daughters. They knew Patrick lived sequestered away in a fortified city with the name of Autism, but now, someone had shown them how to gain access to Patrick's world. And they had enthusiastically entered the gates and had found their brother inside.

Thank You, Lord, for allowing my children to find one another. Help them to continue to grow strong and close. Lead them to cherish and defend each other because You have made each one of them unique and special, I prayed.

I gathered up my brood and headed out the door. On the way home, my daughters chattered about their experiences at the TEACCH Center.

"First, they took us into this big room," Katie said. "Then a lady walked in and started talking to us. Only we did not understand what she was saying. She kept making sounds, and we could tell that she wanted us to do something. But we did not know what she wanted."

"Yeah, she sounded like, 'hyuk, grumm, dawt,'" Emily said.

Sarah giggled.

"Miss Sue told us afterward that she was speaking German!" Katie said.

"She told us Patrick hears words like that," Emily said. "He hears the sounds but doesn't always know what they mean."

I watched Emily's face soften as she spoke about her brother's struggles.

"Tell Mom about the gloves!" Sarah piped in, proud that she was part of the discovery team.

"Well," Emily said. "They took us into another room with tables, and there were pennies all over the tables. They had us put on these big, wooly gloves, and then they told us to pick up the pennies."

"We couldn't do it," Sarah said.

"Have you ever tried to pick up pennies when you had gloves on?" asked Katie, not wanting to be left out of the conversation.

"I don't think I ever have," I said, grinning inwardly.

"Well, it's really hard!" Katie said.

"Why did they make you do that?" I asked.

"They said that's what Patrick feels like when he has to do things with his fingers," Katie said. "They said it's really hard for him when he has to do stuff like button his buttons, write with a pencil, tie his shoes, and cut with scissors. He can't get his fingers to do the things he wants them to do."

A swell of gratitude was building inside of me.

Thank You, Lord, for using the wonderful people at the TEACCH Center to help my daughters better understand their brother, I prayed.

"Ice cream and spinach! Ice cream and spinach!" Sarah announced.

"What about ice cream and spinach?" I asked.

"They helped us understand why Patrick freaks out about certain types of food," Emily said. "They said his tastes are all messed up. Like, he might eat some ice cream, and it would taste like spinach."

"Yuck!" said Sarah, wrinkling up her little button nose and turning her mouth into a grimace.

"Wow!" I said. "That's awful."

"Yeah, and guess what else?" Katie said. "He hears sounds

really loudly. They took us into one room and played this music soooo loudly, and then they told us that Patrick hears sounds that loudly."

"We had to cover our ears," Sarah said, demonstrating with her own hands.

"I bet that's why he goes crazy when we go running around the house making all kinds of noises," Emily said.

"I feel bad for Patrick because so many things are hard for him," Katie said.

"Me, too," Emily said.

"Me, three," said Sarah, quickly joining in.

"Things that are really easy for us are a struggle for him," said Katie, growing unusually still and silent.

For once, I was grateful for the long drive back to China Grove. It was giving us precious time to reflect on the treasure of discoveries uncovered at the TEACCH Center.

"Yes, many things are difficult for Patrick," I said. "But God promises that He causes all things to work together for good for those who love Him and are called according to His purposes. So that means He can take even Patrick's autism and use it for good . . . for Patrick, for each of us, for others. And I think it's teaching all of us to trust Him and to rely on Him, which is a very good thing."

The three girls grew silent as they pondered my words. Patrick continued to doze in his car seat, the rhythm of the road creating a gentle nodding of his head.

What had I learned that day?

A little understanding goes a long way.

How many times had I made a snap judgment about someone based on their outward behavior? How many times had I reacted in frustration or anger, or defined someone as "good" or "bad" without making any attempt to understand what was happening in their life?

Lord, help me to see people as You see them, I prayed as the odometer continued to click the miles toward home.

Patrick's Perspective:

I love my sisters. They mean a lot to me. After that day at the TEACCH Center, they started to understand what I was going through. I feel like they love me and care about me. I am grateful to have such caring sisters.

God taught me that He supplies all my needs according to His riches in glory in Christ Jesus (Philippians 4:19, NASB). God knew I would need lots of support, so He gave me a wonderful family to help me along the way. My dad taught me a lot about being strong and brave, being a man who honors God, and never giving up. He tells me I am his hero. But really, he is mine. He even challenged me to hike Mount Whitney, the highest peak in the continental United States, and we did it— together. (See Chapter 12.) Along the way, I learned to face my fears and be strong, like a man.

And my mom has taught me a lot about God's Word, and she prays with me and reminds me to go to God with all my problems and challenges. She has helped me a lot over the years taking me to therapies, working with teachers, and helping me to be organized, too. And my sisters Katie, Emily, and Sarah and brother-in-law Curt (Katie's husband), and all my relatives, they accept me for who I am, and they love and encourage me all the time. They have been a huge blessing to me.

SOMETHING TO THINK ABOUT:

Are you dealing with someone you do not understand?

What could you do to understand them better?

Would you ask the Lord to help you see people

as He sees them?

Patrick with his sisters (left to right)
Sarah, Katie, and Emily
(Photo by Karen Goforth)

*Patrick with his sisters again
. . . not too sure about the bunnies
(Photo by Karen Goforth)*

*Patrick and the King girls during the
years of countless therapies
(Photo by Karen Goforth)*

SUSAN JANE KING

7

QUITTING WORK

"There is a time for everything,
and everything on earth has its special season."
—Ecclesiastes 3:1, NCV

I gripped the piece of paper in my hand, the paper that would change the course of my life. My resignation letter.

"Is there anything else we need to discuss today?" Jim Freeman said. The chief executive officer of Rowan Regional Medical Center looked across his desk at me, where I sat with Rick Parker, a vice president. The three of us met weekly to talk over issues concerning the public we served.

I loved my job. As the community relations manager, I oversaw marketing and public relations for the burgeoning medical center in Salisbury. I developed far-reaching promotional plans, which I pitched to the board of directors and for which I won support on an ongoing basis. When the press came onsite, I was the one they interviewed on camera and off, my words later appearing in newspaper and TV stories. I wrote news releases and feature stories that appeared in the local media and our own medical publications. I designed and oversaw production of our publications. I managed special events. I frequently spoke in the community. I planned and implemented all of our marketing and advertising efforts. I served on the management team, helping to steer the present and future course of our medical center. It was my dream job.

I looked at Mr. Freeman, the man who had hired me and supported me the past seven years. The man who said he liked to hire thoroughbreds as leaders and let them run. The man who had given me the ability to do exactly that. Our marketing and public relations programs had won awards and improved awareness and public perceptions.

"Yes, there is one more thing," I said. "I want to turn in my resignation."

"No you don't!" Mr. Freeman shot back.

He looked at Rick.

"Do you know anything about this?"

"No, sir," Rick said.

Rick and I had enjoyed an amicable professional relationship the past several years. We respected and supported one another. I reported directly to Rick, and both of us met regularly with Mr. Freeman.

"Why?" asked Mr. Freeman, gaining his composure.

"David and I have prayed about it, and we believe the Lord is calling me to quit work at this point in our lives," I said.

Both men leaned toward me as I continued.

"I believe it has a lot to do with Patrick," I said. "He isn't making progress. He is constantly overwhelmed. His therapies, tests, and treatments require more and more time. Plus, I have three other children and a husband to care for. I want you to know I have loved working here, and I appreciate all the opportunities and support you have given me. My letter says all those things."

I passed the letter across the desk to Mr. Freeman and handed Rick a copy.

I prayed as they read, *Thank You, Lord, for allowing me to experience the kind of job I always wanted. I trust You to lead me on this new part of my life.*

I had come to a fork in the road, and the Lord had directed me to go in an unexpected direction.

From a young age, I felt the career path beckoning me. I loved to write. I filled journals with poetry and stories. I started a family newsletter when I was in elementary and middle school, called the "Mathie Memos." I "published" it several times each month, crammed with stories and updates about the ten members of my immediate family. With everyone's activities and interests, I had a lot to write about.

When I entered high school, I walked into the office of the local newspaper, *The Louisville Herald*, with some writing samples and asked the editor if I could write a weekly column about activities at Louisville High School. "Teen Scene" emerged from that conversation, and I wrote the column until I graduated and left for college. Through my research, I discovered Ohio University in Athens was one of the top-rated schools for journalism, so I journeyed to southern Ohio to major in journalism and public relations.

I was valedictorian of my high school and the E.W. Scripps School of Journalism at Ohio University. I was named "Outstanding Senior Girl" and "Most Likely to Succeed" at Louisville High School, and "Outstanding Senior Graduate" from the E.W. Scripps School of Journalism. I got into public speaking and placed first in the state of Ohio twice and third in the United States in Girls' Extemporaneous Speaking. I worked hard to do my best at everything I attempted. I felt all of it was supposed to lead me to a stellar career and worldly accomplishments.

Until the Lord got hold of me.

Now, sitting there after handing in my resignation letter, all those school and career accomplishments were nothing. I could understand what Paul meant when he said, "Yes, everything else is worthless when compared with the infinite value of knowing Christ Jesus my Lord. For His sake I have discarded everything else, counting it all as garbage, so that I could gain Christ" (Philippians 3:8, NLT).

I knew Jesus, and I understood He loved me. I could trust Him with my life and my future. I knew He would take care of us.

Recently, I had started reading my Bible for the first time in my life. The words seemed to jump off the page straight into my heart. They were full of life, power, encouragement, and direction. I would pick up my Bible whenever I had the time, even closing my office door over my lunch hour to read its treasured words in private.

One day, I arrived early for an interview with a doctor at his office. I sat outside in my car and pulled out my Bible.

"Now, concerning spiritual gifts, brethren, I do not want you to be unaware . . ."

I read through 1 Corinthians 12 and learned about the types of spiritual gifts, how they are given individually by God for the common good of God's people, and how they are meant to build up God's people in caring for one another.

"You will not be able to use your spiritual gift unless you quit work."

The words, whispered to my heart, made me halt my reading.

I have to quit work.

I sensed it in my spirit.

The why and the how were not there yet. Just the what — quit work.

I wrote it across the notepad I had brought for the interview.

"Quit Work."

I walked into the office for the interview with the doctor and gave the receptionist my name. I sat in the patient waiting area, which was beautifully decorated with elegant wallpaper, upholstered chairs, silk flowers, and colorful paintings.

"If you quit work, you won't be able to decorate your home like this."

I startled at the thought.

I added the word "Opposition" to my note-pad and put the words "decorating home" under it.

Later that day, David and I went to a meeting with Patrick's teachers at his preschool. They outlined the extensive help Patrick needed to catch up with his peers.

"You aren't going to be able to afford the help Patrick needs if you quit work."

I added "paying for Patrick's help" to the list.

I went back to work and received word the managers had been called into a special meeting. I walked to the conference room, where I heard about a new bonus system going into effect the next year.

"You are going to miss out on that money if you quit work now."

I added, "Bribery! Making extra money," to the notepad.

Later that night, David found my notepad on the kitchen table.

"What is this about?" he asked.

I told him about my unusual day, and he listened, nodding occasionally.

"Well, it sounds like you need to quit work," he said.

I was ready. I truly trusted the Lord. I would have walked into the CEO's office the next day and quit, if the Lord had told me to do that.

"But we need to pray about the timing," David said.

"Remember how Moses got a sense that the Lord wanted him to deliver the Israelites, but he jumped ahead of God, killing the Egyptian soldier, thinking it was time, that the people would follow him? Moses wound up in the desert for 40 years until God's timing was right." (This story is recounted in Acts 7:20-34.)

I remembered the story from the "Experiencing God" class we had taken on Wednesday nights at church. The class focused on "Knowing and Doing the Will of God." One thing it emphasized was searching for God's will (and timing) through the Bible, prayer, circumstances, and church.iii David and I committed to look for God's timeline in all of those areas.

"Do you think God still gives signs to people?" I asked David one evening as we were getting ready for bed.

"What do you mean?" he asked.

"Well, Gideon asked for a sign with the fleece (Judges 6:36-40), and God even asked Hezekiah what kind of sign he wanted and gave it to him (2 Kings 20:9-11)," I said.

"Yeah, I think God can still give signs if He wants to. Why?" David asked.

"Because I kind of asked Him for one," I said.

David looked at me.

"Well, I am ready to quit work because I know that's what the Lord wants me to do, but I want to get the timing right. I feel a lot of financial responsibility to our family. Kind of like Gideon felt responsible for his men. He did not want to act rashly and jeopardize his men. I don't want to act impulsively and put our family at risk financially. So, I asked God if He wanted me to quit work immediately, to show me a rainbow today."

David raised an eyebrow.

"I didn't see one," I said.

"Well, then, I guess it's not time to quit," David said. "I'm certain that if anyone truly wants to do God's will in God's timing, then God is going to let them know what that is. Let's keep seeking Him."

A few days later, David approached me with our Sunday School lesson book in hand.

"I've got it!" he said. "I know when you are supposed to quit work."

The Sunday School quarterly contained the Bible study lessons for the next quarter at church. He pointed to the table of contents and a lesson scheduled for three months ahead on May 4. It said, "Peter was obedient to what the Lord had called him to do."

"That is supposed to be your last week of work," David said.

I was so glad the Lord had told David. As the leader of our family, he needed to feel confident about the timing of this important decision. The next week, I was in Mr. Freeman's office with my letter of resignation. I wanted to give them as much time as possible to find a replacement.

After overcoming their shock, Mr. Freeman and Rick did what they had been doing my entire career at Rowan Regional. They sought to understand and support me in my decisions.

After my meeting was over, David and I drove to pick up Patrick from daycare and the girls from afterschool care. Ages 4, 6, 8, and 10, they were surprised to see both of us picking them up together.

They squealed with delight when we entered the back door. Colorful streamers and bright balloons decorated the kitchen, and an enormous cake sat in the middle of the table.

"A party! A party!" Sarah said.

"What's the party for?" Katie asked.

The girls trained their eyes on David.

"Well, the Lord has told us that He wants your mom to quit work and stay home with all of you. Today, she told her boss about it. This is a party to celebrate that God is doing something new and special in our lives," David said.

The news slowly registered with the girls.

"Well, now I know there is a God," Katie said, "because I have been praying for this for a long time."

Surprised but happy, I gave her a big hug.

"Let's celebrate!" I said.

I cut the cake and handed out slices to our eager daughters, who had each claimed a balloon for themselves. They went running out on the deck outside our kitchen to eat their cake.

"Mommy! Daddy!" Emily shouted. "You have to come see this!"

David and I stepped outside into the bright sunlight.

We both gasped.

"Why am I surprised?" David said.

He put his arm around me as we both gazed at the

magnificent double rainbow that began in the woods and arched over the top of our house.

Patrick's Perspective:

I don't remember when my mom worked or what it was like, but I do remember what it was like after she quit work. I enjoyed having my mom home with me because I had someone to help, encourage, and talk with me throughout the day. If my mom had been working all the time, I don't feel I would have had the type of constant encouragement I needed. I might not have even graduated high school if I did not have that support. Mom was available to me whenever I needed her. Being autistic, it is easy to get stressed out, but my mom's presence helps make it easier. My dad has helped me, too, encouraging me and enabling me to think about things more clearly. My mom quit work to help me, and my dad kept working to help me. I love them both.

SOMETHING TO THINK ABOUT:

Has your life, under the Lord's direction,

ever taken an unexpected turn?

How do your plans compare to God's plans?

Will you trust the Lord to direct your life?

Do you believe the Lord loves you and will provide for you?

Are you willing to do what the Lord asks,

in the Lord's timing?

*Susan with David and (left to right) Emily, Sarah,
Patrick, and Katie, during Susan's work years at
Rowan Regional Medical Center
(Photo by Karen Goforth)*

8

LEARNING TO TRULY SEE OTHERS

"Do nothing from selfishness or empty conceit,
but with humility of mind regard one
another as more important than yourselves;
do not merely look out for your own personal interests,
but also for the interests of others."
—Philippians 2:3-4, NASB

I recently watched the movie *Avatar*, snuggled up with David on our couch. A futuristic movie set on an alien world with exotic life forms, Avatar features a Marine who enters a community of indigenous people and tries to earn their trust and respect. A recurring phrase throughout the movie is, "I see you." The native people speak the phrase to the natural life forms around them. They share the words with one another. Eventually, the Marine and a local young woman exchange the words after they have had a serious argument.[iv] "I see you." In the movie and in life, the words convey empathy and understanding, the ability to peer deeply into someone else's heart and see the treasure inside.

I encountered my own "I see you" experience on a Wednesday night at church. We were having a Living Christmas Tree, and I took a big step in joining the choir. That meant I had to put Patrick in the nursery while I went to practice every Wednesday night for about 12 weeks. To be honest, it was just a desperate attempt to do something normal.

The experiment didn't work.

77

About three weeks into our practices, I was walking down the hallway to pick up Patrick from the nursery, and I was intercepted by three small children running at full speed and broadcasting to anyone in earshot that "Patrick bit Amy!"

My stomach clenched. Occasionally, Patrick would hit, spit, or bite if people came into his space when he was in one of his zoned-out moments. The sudden sensory invasion would frighten him, and he would react strongly, trying to protect himself.

I had an immediate flashback to his three-year-old Sunday School class. I had walked Patrick into his room, smiling and greeting his two teachers. We were new to the church, and I was hoping to make friends fast, especially with those who would be working with my son. The older woman in the room greeted me coldly and said, "Do you see that little boy over there?" pointing to a cute, blue-eyed, brown-haired cherub, who was pushing a toy truck across the floor.

"Yes," I said.

"Well, your son has bitten him twice. And if he does it again, he will no longer be welcome in this classroom!" she said harshly.

I froze. I had not heard about the biting at all.

"Okay," I said.

I turned Patrick over to the younger, more pleasant woman in the room, who had a look of horror mixed with sympathy on her face, and I left, walking stoically to my own Sunday School classroom.

David appeared a few minutes later, after dropping off our daughters in their classrooms.

My mind had already travelled a long distance down the road of despair.

Why is Patrick having all of these problems? What am I doing wrong as a mother? Why can't I help him? Will other people ever accept him and love him for who he is? Will he be kicked out of Sunday School? Does everyone think I'm a bad parent? I think I'm a bad parent. God help me . . .

"How did it go?" David asked.

That's all it took. A flood of tears erupted, and I fled from our Sunday School classroom, not wanting anyone to see me. I made it about halfway down the hall before running into John, a friend of David's from the choir.

"Susan? What's wrong?" he said.

By then, I was sobbing. The kind of uncontrollable sobs that put your whole body into convulsions. I couldn't stop. I couldn't talk. All the frustrations and pain were finding release through my tears, and I just let them pour out.

I heard footsteps.

"It's okay, John," David said. I felt his arms around me, and I just melted into him. He ushered me off into a side room, and I told him the whole story.

"I don't know what to do!" I said. "I don't know how to help Patrick. And it hurts so badly."

"Shh, shh. It will be okay," said David, willing it to be so.

"Will it?" I said. "Will it ever?"

"Patrick bit Amy!" The words cut their way into my consciousness, interrupting that dark memory.

"Patrick bit Amy!"

I steeled myself for what might greet me when I entered the nursery.

There was Amy, crying and rubbing her arm, the teeth marks still visible and red.

Patrick was in the corner, oblivious. He had a red plastic cup perched on top of a spoon. He was rocking the cup with the spoon and tracking its movements with his eyes.

I knelt down beside Amy. Her mother Elaine had her arms wrapped around her petite, curly-haired daughter.

"Amy, I am so sorry that Patrick hurt you," I said. "What he did was wrong, and I hope you can find it in your heart to forgive him."

Amy stopped crying, looked at me, and haltingly nodded her head yes.

Her mother sat there calmly.

"Elaine, I am so sorry," I said painfully.

"It's okay," she said softly.

No, it's not, I thought. *It's not okay at all! Nothing is okay.*

"Amy, we love you, and we think you are a wonderful little girl," I said with a deep sadness.

I went over and stood near Patrick until he perceived I was there. I showed him the pictures of our van and our home lined up on his Velcro planner so he knew it was time to leave.

Sadness enveloped me as we walked to the car. My shoulders drooped. I wore defeat like a heavy, wet blanket. I believed the lie.

I AM a bad parent. I can't help my son.

Three days later, a card came in the mail. It had Elaine's name in the return address section. My fingers trembled as I tore it open.

I just can't take any more criticism or harsh judgment, I thought. *I really feel like I am at the breaking point!*

"Dear Susan, I want to thank you for the way you comforted my daughter the other night at church. It especially means a lot to me because I know how much you have been hurting about your son. I just want to tell you that I think you are a wonderful mother, and I think you are doing a great job with Patrick. Love, Elaine."

Tears had been my constant companion, and they were flowing again. But this time, they came for a different reason. Elaine's kindness and compassion were allowing waters of hope and streams of healing to flow through my soul. Her encouragement was strengthening me to continue on this unknown road with my son, with my family.

I expected criticism, and I received love and encouragement. I expected resentment, and I found worth. It was God's grace in its purest form because it required sacrifice. Elaine had put her feelings and needs aside and had embraced my world and my experiences. I have never forgotten her kindness, and I have kept her letter all these years. It was a love letter from the Lord sent by one of His faithful servants. It changed my life and gave me hope to keep going. Every time I think of that letter, I ask the Lord, *Please help me to see past myself and to truly see others and what they are experiencing when I am hurt or offended. Help me to be Your voice of love and hope to those who need it.*

In Philippians 2:3-4, NASB, it says, "Do nothing from selfishness or empty conceit, but with humility of mind regard one another as more important than yourselves; do not merely look out for your own personal interests, but also for the interests of others."

That's what Elaine did. She put herself aside and thought about someone else. She looked at me and said, "I see you." The Lord used that moment to teach me a wonderful secret about life. Jesus said, "It is more blessed to give than to receive" (Acts 20:35, NASB). He would know all about that. He gave everything—His very life—for us, and He had joy in the midst of it because He was thinking of us and what it would accomplish for us (Hebrews 12:2,

NASB).

The places of pain in my life have presented the greatest opportunities to learn and to become more like Jesus. I remember the lessons experienced in those places because of the pain involved. Those are the places where I must decide if I am going to trust Jesus and what He says. If I do, He blesses me in amazing ways. That has been my experience. I ask Him to give me eyes to see, ears to hear, and a heart tendered to His voice, because He is the One who sees and hears and loves completely and deeply. He is always saying, "I see you," and we are most like Him when we do the same.

I have had the opportunity to share this truth with my children. When my oldest daughter Katie was a sophomore in high school, Valentine's Day presented a real challenge for her. Ever since she was a little girl, she dreamed of falling in love, getting married, and having a family someday. But Prince Charming hadn't shown up yet; in fact, she didn't even have a boyfriend. At age 16, she didn't want to hear about waiting for the right guy when she was already missing out on being in love. I mean, time was obviously flying by, and old age was just around the corner! Besides, "all the other girls" at school were chatting excitedly about what they were going to do for Valentine's Day with their boyfriends and probably would be getting candy and flowers while Katie had to watch helplessly on the sidelines. That's how she saw it.

"I *hate* Valentine's Day!" she shouted, arriving home from school that day.

I knew why she was upset. She had already told me all about it.

"Katie. I'm going to give you an assignment," I said. "I want you to come up with a plan to do something nice for someone else this Valentine's Day. You aren't the only one who is probably having a hard time with this holiday. Look around, and see what you can come up with."

Katie was dumbfounded.

"But, Mom . . ."

"You have until Friday to come up with a plan," I said. "I am going to ask you then what you have decided to do."

I walked out of the room so she couldn't argue with me.

Friday came, and I didn't even have to ask Katie about it.

"Hey, Mom, do you remember the Bogles? You know, that nice young couple at church who had their first baby a few months ago?" Katie asked.

"Yes, I know them," I said. They were a dear couple who had jumped into helping with the youth at our church even though they were quite busy with careers and a young family. I always appreciated them for that.

"Well, I bet they haven't been out on a date since their baby was born," Katie said. "I think it would be great if I and some of my girlfriends offered to cook them dinner and watch the baby while they went out to the movies on Valentine's Day."

"That is a fantastic idea!" I said.

Putting her usual passion into words, Katie said, "And I thought we could all wear white collared shirts and black pants and even serve them dinner after cooking it. I found some romantic music we could play, and I thought we could put some pretty flowers on the table too."

Katie enlisted two girlfriends to help her. It turned out that "all the other girls" did not have dates after all. When she came back home after her night's adventure, she couldn't stop talking.

"This was the best Valentine's Day ever!" she said. "We had so much fun. The Bogles were very grateful and kept thanking us over and over for giving them a date night. And that baby was adorable!"

"You've learned a very important lesson," I told Katie. "God knows what He is talking about. It is more blessed to give than to receive. Remember that the next time you are upset about something. See if there is some way you can give to others in that situation."

Katie paused reflectively. "Okay. I will."

I have found that I am most unhappy when I am dwelling on me—my hurts, my needs, what I deserve. I am happiest and find great joy when I can do something to help someone else, when I can think about them and find a way to bless them. The Lord shows me things I can do, and I get to do them with Him. Sometimes, He lets me see the results, and we have a big celebration together. Other times, I find my happiness and joy trusting the results to Him.

Patrick's Perspective:

The members of my church have encouraged me so much. And I know they have been praying for me over the years. They have encouraged my family, too. I am grateful for the lady who sent my mom that note. Mom still has that letter, and that was 16 years ago. I am thankful that the people at church have been a family to my family . . . because I was not the only one who needed encouragement. The people in my mom's Sunday School class, especially, have been extremely kind. They talk to me and encourage me and pray for me, too. That means a lot.

SOMETHING TO THINK ABOUT:

Are you sad, discouraged?

Why not ask the Lord to show you

someone you can bless in His name?

Whom might the Lord be asking

you to "see" right now?

*Patrick would hit, spit, or bite when others came
into his space unexpectedly
(Photo by Karen Goforth)*

SUSAN JANE KING

9

CHOOSING TO BE THANKFUL

*"In everything give thanks;
for this is God's will for you in Christ Jesus."
—1 Thessalonians 5:18, NASB*

Life presents so many challenges for Patrick. Every day, he faces mountains to climb and hurdles to jump. Some people might choose to be angry or bitter because of these countless obstacles. Not Patrick. As the years passed, I noticed a startling development. Patrick was continually *choosing to be thankful*, to be exceedingly grateful for the smallest things. He even *looked* for reasons to be thankful.

We carted him everywhere for therapies. Forty minutes to Salisbury and back. An hour to Concord and back. Two hours for the roundtrip to Charlotte. I reasoned that if they had frequent flyer miles for motorists, I would be a platinum level member!

Twice a day, I made the trip to Salisbury so Patrick could be part of a special classroom designed to prepare him for kindergarten. Twice a week, we drove to Concord for occupational therapy. Once a week, we drove to the TEACCH Center. And twice a week, we drove to the University of North Carolina at Charlotte for perceptual motor development training.

The UNCC sessions presented the greatest challenge because they were late in the afternoon, which meant I had to pick up the three girls from school and take them with us. We would sequester ourselves in a classroom somewhere in the building while the

UNCC students worked with Patrick and tried to help him improve his coordination. Those were long days. The girls usually were extremely tired from a full day at school, and I ran myself ragged trying to keep them on task with their homework while squeezing in dinner and driving.

One day, we all walked out to the van after Patrick's session and discovered I had locked my keys in the car.

"Oh no!" I said.

I felt like sinking to the ground in exhaustion. It had been an unusually trying day. The sun had begun its descent toward the horizon, and a cold November wind blew its way through my coat.

I called David, who was 35 miles away at work.

"I've got patients lined up for several hours ahead," he said. His busy optometry practice had blessed us in meeting the numerous financial obligations associated with Patrick's autism.

"We've got AAA. Could you call them? They probably could get there quicker than I could anyway."

Always practical, David served as my rock of reason and pillar of strength as I rowed through a mother's tumultuous emotions in regard to Patrick. David was right. I hung up and called AAA.

"It will be about 90 minutes until we can have someone there," the attendant told me. "Stay near your car so we can find you."

"Ugh!" I thought as I hung up the phone. "Now what?!"

I didn't want to bother David again and make him reschedule a bunch of patients. Plus, it was getting close to rush hour.

"I'm hungry," Patrick said.

Since he had found his words, he had gotten better and better at communicating his needs. I was grateful and frustrated at the same time.

"Me, too," the girls echoed.

"Well, I wonder if we could have pizza delivered to a street corner!" I said jokingly. Then, I thought, "Why not?"

I called information and got the phone number of the Domino's Pizza nearest to campus.

"Can you deliver to a street corner?" I asked.

"Excuse me?" said the young man at the other end of the phone.

"I've got four hungry children. We're locked out of my car. And the locksmith can't get here for an hour and a half. Can you deliver a pizza to University Road near the entrance to the Cone parking deck?

"Uhh, I'll have to check with my manager," he said, surprised.

While the on-hold music bounced off my eardrums, I thought, "I have never been so desperate for a pizza in all of my life!"

"We can do it! We'll be there in 30 minutes," the young man announced.

I gathered up my brood of baby chicks and gave them strict instructions to follow their mother hen. Holding hands, we walked down the parking deck ramps to the street, where I instructed the girls to drop their bookbags in the grass and sit on top of them. Patrick had brought his own backpack along, so he obeyed my directions as well.

About 30 minutes later, we were experiencing the delights of crispy pepperoni, melted mozzarella cheese, spicy marinara sauce, and chewy crust.

"Life is great!" Patrick said.

What?! I thought, barely able to feel my backside because I did not bring a backpack.

Then, I looked at my son.

A huge smile exploded across his face as he munched on what he considered to be life's greatest food product.

He was right.

We were safe. We were together. We were eating.

Life is great.

An hour later, we were packed into our van heading home. And we had a new memory that we would reclaim from the recesses of our minds and talk about for years.

"In everything, give thanks; for this is God's will for you in Christ Jesus" (1 Thessalonians 5:18, NASB). Why would God want us to be thankful in everything?

From watching Patrick, I have realized that being thankful shows that we trust God, that we believe He is in charge, that we rely on Him to bring good out of each and every situation. Being thankful acknowledges that God is in control, that He loves us, and that He is God and we are not. Thankfulness comes from a sense of humility. Not the attitude of "I deserve," but the attitude of "I appreciate." Patrick says thank you more than anyone I know, and he reminds me to be thankful every day. For that, I am grateful.

Patrick's Perspective:

God has taught me that He knows the plans He has for me. Plans to prosper me and not to harm me, to give me a future and a hope (Jeremiah 29:11, NASB). I have learned that God made me autistic, and He has good plans with that. He says I am "fearfully and wonderfully made" (Psalm 139:14, NASB). For a long time, I did not like being autistic—being different. I tried to be "normal" like everyone else. But I know now that God made me who I am. And He has His own plans and reasons for how He made me. I hope people can see how great He is through my autism and my struggles. Because He is great. And nothing is impossible with Him. I am very thankful when I and others can experience who God is through my autism. And every day, I am more and more thankful, as God helps me and helps others through me.

SOMETHING TO THINK ABOUT:

What could you thank God for today?

Where are you challenged to trust God?

Would you choose to trust Him in that situation,

thanking Him for His presence in it?

How might God use your present situation to help others?

Would you trust Him to do that?

Would you follow His leading in doing so?

Consider starting a "thankfulness journal." Write in it something

you are thankful for each day. Try writing a thank you note once

each week to someone for whom you are thankful.

At a young age, Patrick chose
to be thankful continually

10

FINDING GOD IN THE DARK TIMES

"If I say, 'Surely the darkness will overwhelm me,
and the light around me will be night,'
even the darkness is not dark to You,
and the night is as bright as the day.
Darkness and light are alike to You."
—Psalm 139:11-12, NASB

I rolled over in bed for about the tenth time. Anguish filled my soul.

I can't! I can't! I can't keep going this way!

I felt the weight of the world on my shoulders. Actually, it was on my chest, and it was crushing me. I felt like one of those carnival plate spinners. The kind who have long, flexible sticks in their hands, and who place plates on the end of the sticks. They have to keep moving the sticks to keep the plates spinning. If they stop, the plates come crashing to the ground. I just didn't feel like I could keep my plates spinning anymore.

I had been here before.

Several years ago, I had experienced the same unwelcome feelings of anxiety, stress, and depression. I was working at Rowan Regional Medical Center, putting in 40-60 hours per week. I had four small children, all of whom needed time, attention, and care. Plus, I had lots of issues with Patrick and no answers. I was involved in some community organizations that required my attention. I had commitments at church. And last, but certainly not least, David, my dear husband, was getting the scraps of my time. I felt this distance growing between us, and I didn't know how to fix it. My parents had divorced when I was 30, and it had devastated me. My own insecurities made me ponder the same possibilities for my marriage. What if David wasn't happy being married to me anymore? What if he left me? What if I ruined my children because I neglected to give them enough time and attention? What if I crashed and burned at my job?

I thought about how exhausted and miserable I was, and then the darkness of the night seemed to press even closer.

"Why don't you just kill yourself?" an ugly voice pressed. "You're a failure on every level, and everyone would be better off without you. There's a razor in the bathroom . . ."

I shivered, shocked that my thoughts had gone in that direction.

David was sleeping soundly beside me. I wanted to shake him awake, to ask him to help me.

But I didn't.

Somehow, I had bought into the lie that I had to be strong and take care of everything at home and at work. I shouldn't bother David. I had to fix things myself. Besides, if I talked with him, he might just confirm my worst fears—that he was disappointed in me and didn't care for me anymore.

Lord, please wrap Your arms around me, and let me know how much You love me, because I feel all alone in the world, I prayed. I eventually fell into a fitful sleep.

I rolled out of bed the next morning, dazed from the lack of sleep. I groggily entered the kitchen and began fixing breakfast for the girls. Suddenly, all the heaviness from the night before found me and enveloped me like a heavy cloak.

At that moment, Sarah burst into the room, and said, "Mommy, Mommy, I just have to hug you right now!" She flung her sweet little 3-year-old arms around me and said, "Mommy, you are the bestest mommy in the whole world, and I don't want you to die."

I caught my breath.

In that instant, I remembered my prayer from the night before. And as I felt those precious arms around me, I thought, "He's real! And He cares about me!" I realized I was not alone, and I never had been.

Within a week of my "hug from God," a friend shared with me the following Bible verse: "It is by grace that you have been saved, and that is not of yourselves. It is a gift from God, not of works, so that no one may boast" (Ephesians 2:8-9, NASB). That verse broke open a world of understanding to me. I realized I did not have to "work." I did not have to do anything to earn God's love. I did not have to be the perfect mother, the perfect wife, the perfect employee, the perfect friend. He loved me. Period. He loved me so much that He sent His son Jesus to die on the cross to pay the penalty for my sins so I would not have to. That's love. That's a gift. I did not earn it. He chose to give it. I just had to believe it and receive it.

I felt the weight of the world leave. I was free! And I have been free ever since.

No matter how dark times may seem, the Lord's love overrides it all. Everything is light to Him. He sees everything, knows everything, and orchestrates everything. We don't have to "work" because He is always working, and He has us in His loving care at all times. How freeing!

I wish that night had been the only time in my life when I battled depression. It wasn't. Here I was in another season of depression when life had overwhelmed me once again. I knew I didn't have to "work" to earn the Lord's love, acceptance, and approval. I had learned that lesson from the first time. But this time, the Lord wanted to teach me another powerful lesson: His Word helps me fight my battles.

I was curled up in bed, feeling like I had a heavy, wet blanket pressing down on me. Its weight paralyzed me. I could not get up and out of the bed. Suddenly, a scripture I had read months before came to mind: "These are the nations that the Lord left in the land to test those Israelites who had not experienced the wars of Canaan. He did this to teach warfare to generations of Israelites who had no experience in battle" (Judges 3:1-2, NLT).

I sensed the Lord telling me He was allowing this depression to come at me so that I would learn how to fight spiritually. Then, I felt Him urging me, "I did not make myself known to you for you to lie immobilized in this bed. Get up and fight!"

I jumped, startled by the message. Then, I started willing myself to push past the heavy weight pressing against me. I forced myself to put my feet on the floor and stand. As soon as I did, countless Bible verses began flooding my mind. Scriptures about God's power, my ability to stand and overcome through Jesus, the greatness of God, and His love for me. I began speaking them out loud as they came to mind, personalizing them to my life: "I can do all things through Christ who strengthens me" (Philippians 4:13). "I am more than a conqueror through Christ who loves me" (Romans 8:37). "God has said He will never leave me or forsake me, so I am going to confidently say, 'The Lord is my Helper. I will not be afraid'" (Hebrews 13:5-6). "I am going to find my joy in You, Lord, and I am going to praise your name!" (Psalm 9:2).

As the words continued to flow from my lips, the heaviness rolled away from me. Joy and peace took its place.

The Bible tells us God's Word is living and active (Hebrews 4:12). God's Spirit and His life-giving power flow in and through His Word (John 6:63). His Word moved that day to break the chains of my depression. His truth sliced through the lies that bound me with despair. Maybe that's why God's Word is called a sword (Ephesians 6:17). Over the years, the Lord has continued to instruct and guide me in wielding the sword of His Word. It serves as a powerful weapon in slaying the monsters of fear, anxiety, depression, and defeat.

Patrick's Perspective:

I get depressed sometimes, too. It happens often. When I have a lot going on, when the schedule gets rearranged and I lose that structure, when somebody says hurtful things to or about me, and when I do not do as well as I want to, a heaviness sets into my heart and chest.

In the fall of my freshman year in high school, both of my pets died—my dog Maggie and my cat Shadow. I loved those pets, and they had been part of my life for 12-14 years. At the same time, I had feelings for a girl, and I saw her making some bad life choices and kissing other boys, too. I had two best friends, Angel and Alex. Angel moved away to another city about an hour away, and Alex went to the other high school in southern Rowan County. I felt lonely and depressed. My parents were so concerned that they took me to a counselor. It really helped to talk with someone about what I was feeling.

Later that month, I sat down and read a lot of Bible verses, and God used them to encourage me. God's Word comforts me when I feel bad, and I like to read it. I believe the things He tells me about Himself and life in the Bible. When I read the Bible, pray, and choose to believe and praise God, I can feel the depression lifting out of my heart and chest.

In college, I have talked with the university counselor as well as professors and other staff members when I feel depressed or overwhelmed. I also talk with my parents when I feel stressed or sad, and they help me process my feelings and sometimes even assist me with developing a plan to deal with my issues.

I feel like exercise also relieves my stress. I can feel pretty down, but once I get in the pool and swim my laps, I feel better. I want to remain active so I can continue to have a good attitude about things.

SOMETHING TO THINK ABOUT:

Are you feeling the "weight of the world" on your shoulders?

Would you transfer that weight onto the Lord?

He can handle it!

Are you trying to be "perfect"?

Would you accept that the Lord is perfect,

so you don't have to be?

Imagine the Lord's loving arms wrapped around you at this very

moment. Thank Him for the way He tenderly cares for you.

Would you consider reading your Bible the next time

you feel depressed? The Psalms contain lots of material

for redirecting your focus to God. Try Psalm 43:5 and Psalm

62:1, 5-8. Lamentations 3:21-26 also offers great

encouragement in difficult times.

Is there someone you could talk to about how you feel?

Could you use exercise as a way to relieve your stress?

(If you have underlying health issues, you should check with your doctor

first before starting an exercise program.)

11

NAVIGATING THE MARRIAGE WATERS

*"For this cause a man shall leave his father and mother,
and shall cleave to his wife;
and the two shall become one flesh. This mystery is great;
but I am speaking with reference to Christ and the church."*
—*Ephesians 5:31-32, NASB*

God created marriage. In it, He calls a man to leave the family where he grew up and create a new family with his wife. After the Lord, a man's relationship with his wife should be most important. He is to cleave to his wife (stick to her like glue) and to become one flesh with her (united physically, emotionally, and spiritually).

When marriage exists as God designed, a husband and wife operate as one unit under the Lord's care and leadership. The marriage should represent how Jesus and His people relate to one another (Ephesians 5:31-32).

Having a special-needs child can threaten any marriage. In fact, although the divorce/separation rate for first time marriages in the United States ranges from 40 to 50 percent, the divorce rate for parents of children with autism spectrum disorders is said to be as high as 80 percent.[v]

Why? In addition to the normal challenges encountered by married couples, autism adds a variety of new stresses: emotional, financial, and physical. Care for the child can become all-consuming and exhausting, while the marriage dies from neglect.

When people feel threatened and overwhelmed, one of two

instincts generally tend to kick in: fight or flight. I could never thank the Lord enough for giving me a husband who chose to fight — for his son, his family, his marriage — instead of running from the pain and added responsibilities.

My husband David is an Iron Man — literally. He competes in events where triathletes have to swim 2.4 miles, bike 112 miles, and run a full marathon (26.2 miles), all in the same day. He's strong physically. Yet, I see him as an Iron Man on the spiritual level, too. Once the Lord came into his life (just one month before I had my salvation experience), he became iron-clad serious about serving Him. So when we got Patrick's diagnosis, David plunged into renewing his commitment to me and our family out of his dedication to the Lord.

Recently, I asked him how he thought Patrick's autism had affected our marriage and family. He said, "As with any child, having an autistic or special needs child makes you less self-centered. You have to focus on helping someone else, and that is a good thing. I think it has made our entire family more team focused."

If our family is a team, then David is the coach.

I love watching David teach and train all our children, but especially our son. Patrick means "strong," and David calls forth the strength in him.

"That's why I wanted him to hike Mt. Whitney with me," David said. (See Chapter 12.) "I wanted him to realize he could break through barriers and do something he thought he couldn't do. Patrick told me he was afraid on that trip, and I told him, 'Being afraid doesn't mean you're not a man. When you're afraid, you hike afraid. When you're tired, you take another step.' I want Patrick to see he can be strong and stand for what's right in this world. I am not just concerned about his personal accomplishments; I care about the kind of man he is becoming."

David had a plaque made years ago that hangs in our hallway upstairs. It says, "We will never do it perfectly around here, but we will always do it together." When it comes to our family, no man gets left behind with David leading. And no woman, for that matter, which especially reassures me.

After my parents' divorce, insecurity gripped me with a vise-like fear. If my parents could divorce, then what about us?

When I finally talked with David about my insecurities, he

reassured me. "I'm not going anywhere . . . and it's not because of you."

I looked at him, confused.

"It's because I fear God. I know I am going to be accountable to Him someday for the type of husband and father I have been," David said.

I could feel my concerns fade away, like the shadows disappear when the sun comes up. I didn't have to worry about trying to hold on to my husband. The Lord was keeping him right where He wanted him.

David and I are very different. He is extremely athletic, and I am, well . . . not. I was always the last one picked for kickball in grade school. If adults played that game, I still would be chosen last. A born leader, David blazes trails and inspires people wherever he goes. He serves on several boards and committees, which value his foresight and wisdom. I, however, am content sipping on a cup of tea while talking with a friend, reading a good book, or writing.

David sees the big picture and plans for the future. I take care of the day-to-day details. David plays the guitar and sings beautifully. I have been told singing is not my gift . . . by my giggling children when I try to sing the high notes. I, however, love to pore over my Bible and teach a weekly adult Sunday School class about the treasures in God's Word. David doesn't like to sit still to do all that studying.

Our personalities differ, too. David is passionate, strong, and direct. He seeks to get results, to get things done. I'm sensitive and extremely tender-hearted. My feelings get wounded easily, and I hurt quickly for others. With Patrick, David has concerns about Patrick in the long-term: Will Patrick be able to make a living? Will he be able to support and nurture a family? Will he lead and do the hard things, while not being influenced to compromise by the public or his peers?

As Patrick's mom, I just want to give him a hug when he feels anxious, sad, or fearful. I listen to him and pray with him about his many day-to-day struggles, and I ask him questions to try to help him learn how to problem-solve. David helps me not to mother Patrick too much and to look at the big picture, and I help David to listen, encourage, and manage the day-to-day issues so he can give his wonderful advice to a receptive son. We make a good team.

We didn't always feel that way. We experienced many long, lonely years after Patrick's diagnosis where we felt disconnected from one another and overwhelmed by our responsibilities. We often viewed our differences as flaws instead of unique attributes chosen by God. The Bible says each person on earth is God's workmanship (Ephesians 2:10); that means every one of us is uniquely crafted by the Lord.

He wisely and lovingly chooses and gives us our personalities, temperaments, abilities, physical traits, strengths, and weaknesses. He weaves all those features together to create one-of-a-kind individuals, who carry and represent His attributes on earth. We are made in His image (Genesis 1:26), and the Lord says His designs are meant to fulfill His special purposes (Ephesians 2:10). Even in marriage.

Like a beautiful tapestry, the threads of our individual lives can come together in a marriage and create a beautiful work of art that would not have existed without the intertwining strands. In the process, the Lord can display a stronger picture of Himself through the combined lives of husband and wife. Ultimately, the tapestry becomes one stunning picture of Jesus, versus a bunch of individual threads. Growing and becoming one in marriage takes time and commitment, and the Lord helps in the process.

Over the years, David and I have come to respect what each of us brings to our marriage. The Lord has done great things through our being together—much more than could have been accomplished separately. We are stronger collectively than we are individually. The Lord has taught us that marriage is not about what we can get, but about what we can give—to our spouse, and especially to God, by cooperating with Him in what He is trying to accomplish in and through our union.

Sure, we have had our ups and downs. My parents never fought in front of me and my siblings, and David's parents never hesitated to express themselves. I was crushed when David would use his strong voice with me, trying to solve problems, and he was frustrated when I would not talk about things that bothered me. We have had to work through these issues, and we continue to do so. When it comes to our children, we have had to learn how to communicate our concerns and opinions in a manner that suits our spouse's personality.

I have had to accept David's involvements and commitments outside the home as part of what makes him uniquely David. He has had to realize and accept I just don't like and often struggle with keeping up the family budget and cleaning the house. We each have come to love and respect the unique individual we married.

We also learned to intentionally carve out time together, scheduling dates on our family calendar. We discovered life would steal our time and devotion to one another if we didn't fight for it. Whether we went out to breakfast together or cuddled on the couch watching a movie, we tried to commit to spending date moments with one another each week. Friends and family members were willing to help us keep this commitment, often assisting with childcare arrangements. I discovered I needed to avoid discussing family problems and concerns during these dates, so David and I could focus on one another. Then, we would get back to business after our date was over.

In light of Patrick's challenges and our other responsibilities as parents, we reprioritized our family. David quit playing golf. He stopped his involvement with the local theater, and he stepped down from being a member of several civic organizations. I withdrew from some clubs as well and eventually felt led to quit work. We worked through those decisions together.

From the time of Patrick's diagnosis, David said, "We are not going to use Patrick's perceived disability as an excuse for him not to try. Everybody has insecurities and challenges. It's what we do in the midst of them that defines who we are. We are going to hold out the picture of a bright future in front of Patrick and let him know we believe he has it in him to accomplish great things."

David's casting a vision for success helped me many times when I just wanted to grab my son and hide him away somewhere when the world seemed especially cruel and judgmental. David would always rally the family during those times, encouraging us to ignore the misconceptions of others and keep moving forward.

This growth in our marriage came through the Lord's intervention. He directed us to some wonderful Christian counselors, who helped us unpack our family baggage and see one another through the eyes of Jesus. Fortunately, we chose wise counselors because they can have great influence — for good or bad (Proverbs 24:6 and 1 Corinthians 15:33).

Being married is like sailing a ship. Sometimes the waters are smooth and calm, and other times, you are fighting huge waves and gale-force winds. Either way, the goal is to navigate together and allow Jesus to captain the ship. Whenever David and I have conflicts, the best solution is always to go to the Lord about it. He knows the best course to take.

I remember the time He told me to stop expecting David to be Jesus . . . I was putting too many unrealistic expectations on him and needed to show him some grace instead. I also remember when David humbly approached me and said the Lord had instructed him to treat me more gently, and he was going to try to do so. Only the Lord is able to look straight into the heart of issues and give the perfect advice and direction. Jesus doesn't come to take sides in marriage conflicts. He comes to take over.

As David and I grew in our marriage, the Lord ultimately arranged circumstances so that we got baptized together on our 12th anniversary: December 15, 1996. I felt as if the Lord was telling us then, as He is today, "Okay. Just remember: We are in this together."

The Bible says, "Though one may be overpowered, two can defend themselves. A cord of three strands is not quickly broken" (Ecclesiastes 4:12, NASB). In marriage, Jesus is the third strand, the main cord that keeps the marriage together and strong. It's our job as husband and wife to wrap our individual cords around Him. He actively works to help the marriage not only survive, but also thrive. After all, since marriage is supposed to represent how Christ and the church relate to one another, He has a vested interest in making marriage all it can be, a vehicle of love and respect for the world to see.

I know only the Lord could take two different people like me and David, give us four beautiful children, and teach us how to raise each one of them, while caring for one another in the process. Our marriage has blossomed like a tender rose, opening its fragrant petals in the light of the Lord's love. Or . . . Our marriage has grown stronger and achieved God's intended greatness, like a triathlete, pushing through each challenge and celebrating the triumphs only the Lord could have made possible. (You pick the version you prefer!)

Patrick's Perspective:

I am happy Mom and Dad have taken care of me. I really look up to them. I hope to raise a family in the future, and I want to be an inspiration to my children like my parents are to me. My mom and dad are unique individuals, who stay true to their personalities. I like how they stay true to themselves, how God made them, and still have a good marriage. They make a lot of sacrifices for my sisters and me. Even though I am not ready just yet, I would like to be a husband and father someday. I am trusting God will find the right person for me.

SOMETHING TO THINK ABOUT:

Do you know of a marriage that represents the love and

respect between Christ and His church?

What makes that marriage so special?

Has your life been impacted by someone's marriage?

What can you learn from that experience?

Are you married? If so, will you allow Jesus to take

over in making it all it can be?

If you are married, how might the Lord be

using your differences for good?

What might the Lord be trying to accomplish in and through

your marriage? In and through the marriages of your friends?

How can you pray for them?

What are some steps you can take to prioritize your marriage and family or other important relationships?

What can you do to personally encourage married couples you know?

*Susan and David
at their wedding*

Susan and David today

12

HIKING THE TRAIL TO MANHOOD

"He told our fathers to teach their children."
—Psalm 78:5, NLV

As we listened to the rhythmic hum of the luggage turnstiles, Patrick handed me a small scrap of paper.

"Grandpa gave me this," he said. "Whenever it was hard, I would look at it."

It was crumpled and smudged with dirt, reflecting the events of the past seven days: "So do not fear, for I am with you; do not be dismayed, for I am your God. I will strengthen you and help you; I will uphold you with my righteous right hand" (Isaiah 41:10, NIV).

"I want to put it up in my room," Patrick said.

"Whenever it was hard . . ."

I knew it was going to be difficult. When my husband's father announced in December 2006 that he wanted all the King men to hike to the top of Mount Whitney in California, I was surprised. Not about my stalwart 74-year-old father-in-law Don King, or his daring sons, Don Jr., age 50, Doug, age 48, and my husband David, age 46, at that time. I was surprised—and a little frightened—that they had included Patrick, the only grandson, in their plans.

"It will be awesome to have three generations on the top of that mountain," David had said.

"Yes, it would," I said, thinking to myself, *How in the world is that going to happen?!*

With the highest peak in the continental United States, Mount Whitney juts up to a pinnacle of 14,505 feet high. It's located in the Sierra Nevada mountain range of California. Their planned hike was supposed to take 5 days, June 30 through July 4.

"Some of the people who try to hike to the peak don't make it," David told me.

That's because the mountain presents several challenges: high altitude that could make you physically sick, lower oxygen levels (20 percent less than at sea level), extremely rugged terrain, rock slides, and the elements of nature. The hikers would have to go 42 miles uphill, with over 12,000 feet of uphill and downhill elevations. That's a distance equal to going to the bottom of the Grand Canyon and back up two and a half times, and they were going to do it while carrying 40- to 60-pound packs, sleeping in tents, filtering their water from streams, going to the bathroom outdoors, and bringing and cooking their own food.

Then there was Patrick, and his autism.

I thought about Patrick's special makeup in light of the challenges and demands of the trip.

First, he didn't like certain tastes and textures. As a result, he had a very limited diet. What would he eat on the trip?

The next few months, David let Patrick try a variety of dehydrated foods that you add water to, cook over a fire, and eat. Patrick settled on a lasagna product he could tolerate. They found a strawberry cereal bar for breakfast and a beef stick and cheese for lunch that he would eat, too.

"He can eat the same thing for all his meals," David said. "That's not going to bother him, as long as he can eat it."

Patrick has an acute sense of hearing. What was he going to do with the sounds of the crickets at night, the rustling of leaves, etc.?

Patrick experiences pain at higher levels than most people. How would he handle the rigors of the trail?

Patrick needs routine. The unpredictable rocks his world. Who knew what was going to happen on the hike? If he gets what we call "sensory overload," he has to detach, and he usually retreats to his room. On the trail, there would be no place to hide.

"He needs this, Susan. He's becoming a man, and he needs to learn what it means to be a man," David said.

Patrick was 14 at the time, but in a lot of ways, he seemed much younger. He had this innocent quality, a sweetness and sincerity you didn't find in a lot of teenage boys. Unlike other autistics, he was in tune with other people's feelings. I had heard him tell his sister Sarah a few months before, "It hurts my heart when you're sad."

Lord, please let me know if Patrick is supposed to do this. It frightens me. I'm a mother and a wife, and I just want everyone to be safe, I prayed. Over time, I sensed His leading to let Patrick go. Still, I resisted.

So he needs to learn about being a man. Well, why can't David just take him in the shop and build something, or go fishing for a day, or practice getting lost and not asking for directions?

But then I remembered a book David had read several years ago called "Wild at Heart," which talked about a man's need for adventure.[vi]

I also remembered James Dobson's study, "Bringing Up Boys," in which he emphasized that mothers should allow the fathers to take the lead role in their sons' lives, "to show them how to be men" once they reach the end of the pre-teen years, and beyond.[vii] I had to let David show Patrick how to be a man. He was the only one in the family who could teach him that important lesson.

"Okay, but please make sure a bear doesn't get him," I said.

David put his hand on my shoulder and said softly, "I won't let anything happen to him."

The next six months, David and Patrick trained for the hike. They went out several times each week and walked 4 to 6 miles with 30- to 40-pound packs strapped on their backs. They even jogged sometimes. They rehearsed setting up the tent. They practiced eating the food. They mapped out a route through downtown China Grove and the vicinity that included several hills. Patrick learned to experience being uncomfortable, smelly, and dirty.

Typical of self-conscious teenagers, Patrick's sisters would say after David and Patrick returned from hiking through town, "I hope nobody knows you're related to us!" Undaunted, David and Patrick kept walking. Finally, the day of the big adventure arrived.

When I dropped them off at the airport in Charlotte on June 29, I decided to grab hold of my own Bible verse: "When I'm afraid, I will put my trust in You" (Psalm 56:3, NASB). I repeated it many times during the next week.

David, Patrick, and Patrick's grandpa and uncles wrote in journals during their hike. The following excerpts are from their journal entries.

***

Day 1: Saturday, June 30

"5:20 a.m. We made it to Lone Pine, where we will start our journey. I am struck by the sheer majesty of the Sierras. The mountains rise straight out of the desert and reach toward the heavens. Patrick has done well thus far. He handled the flight and drive with 'autistic purpose.' 'How long until . . .' was the theme of the day. He has fit in quite well and has already picked up some 'manly terms' from the rest of us. Today will be a great test. We are all a bit anxious about starting at 10,000 feet and hiking the pass today. The altitude and trail could very well take its toll on any of us. This will be an awesome day. A lot of questions will be answered. Memories will be made. My son will experience the most difficult physical experience of his life. And best of all, we'll be together." —David

"We started our journey at 10:10 a.m. I wasn't doing so good because of the altitude! I was getting murdered and felt like moose droppings! I couldn't breathe. Our hike was finished at 5:30 p.m. 7 hours and 20 minutes. I woke up in the middle of the night thinking I heard a moose outside our tent, but it was Dad snoring! I wonder if Mom knows he snores like that!" —Patrick

"We made it to 11,500 feet and are camping at a series of high level lakes. What a day! Patrick survived—barely! It is very difficult to do anything at this altitude, let alone hike with a pack. I am so proud of how he tries. What a heart he has! It was an emotional day. I was so proud of Patrick, but concerned thinking we may not make it. If we make it over New Army Pass tomorrow—12,500 feet—we have a pretty good shot at making it to the summit. I really don't know if we will make it or not. Honestly, it will be a struggle. I miss my family, but I am thanking God for this opportunity." —David

"We've all realized that this is going to take longer than we thought. We have to go more slowly than we anticipated. I've hiked and led hiking trips for years, and I'm a little anxious that we might be in over our heads. But, with God's help, we will continue on as planned. We've already discussed redistributing the pack weights. Dave, Doug, and I are carrying about 60 pounds each. Hopefully, that will make it easier on Dad and Patrick to have lighter packs. Tomorrow is the point of no return. Once we climb to New Army Pass, the only way out is by hiking over 13,650 feet (to Trail Crest on day 5) or by helicopter. At some points on the trail, even the helicopters won't be able to reach us." —Don Jr.

Day 2: Sunday, July 1

"We made it over New Army Pass! It was incredibly hard—like doing a stair climber machine for 7 hours with a bag over your head, with 60-pound weights on your back, and a sunlamp shining on you the whole time. I have never been more proud of Patrick. He hiked 2,000 feet of very difficult switchbacks. I was dying, and he hung right in there. We all feel like he has a good shot at the summit. I'm enjoying sitting up and talking with my brothers at night. We strategize about the next day and have some meaningful conversations about life. Patrick just informed me that I 'stink'! We all stink after hiking in the hot sun for two days without a bath or deodorant. I can't imagine how we're all going to smell after the end of the hike! I've told Patrick at the end of the trail when we come down from the mountain, there is a wonderful little shop that will make him the biggest hamburger he's ever seen—2 pounds! He's taken that hamburger as a 'focal point' for making it (along with Grandpa's Bible verse)!" —David

"Well, we started at 8 a.m. and ended at 3:15 p.m. 7 hours and 15 minutes. The high route scared me because it was narrow, and we were close to the edge. There were rocks all over the trail. I am afraid of heights. I told Dad I was afraid. He told me he understood but that I needed to hike afraid. So I did. I just stared down that mountain and kept going. And guess what?—I made it! I went fast downhill. It was cool." —Patrick

"We all have a dull headache from the altitude. We have to pump water and filter it every chance we get for drinking, cooking, and cleaning up. It has been unseasonably hot, and some of the water holes on the map simply aren't there. Patrick got fired up going down the mountains. He and Uncle Doug love to lead. I just kept one foot in front of the other." —Don Sr.

Day 3: Monday, July 2

"Well, we hiked, and it was the easiest so far. Mosquitoes were everywhere! It was mosquito madness! We wore nets over our heads and gloves on our hands. Our long-sleeved shirts and pants protected the rest of us. Once, I looked at my arm, and I bet there were 50 mosquitoes on my shirt! We started at 8 a.m. and ended at 2:50 p.m. 6 hours and 50 minutes. So easy! Three more days until I get that hamburger! When Dad and I finished hiking, we went fishing and caught a golden trout. That was the first fish I ever caught, and it was beautiful! I also saw marmots today. They look kind of like a groundhog and squirrel mixed together. They're funny!" —Patrick

"When we came downhill out of New Army Pass, Dad really struggled. Going downhill was extremely hard on his knees. He was using his walking poles much like a walker. He had to brace himself with every step downhill. It was gut-wrenching watching how hard it was for him. He was in so much pain. I've always admired and respected my dad, but that moment grew my respect of him even more. He is Korean Vet tough! It was a side of my dad I've never seen before. He was tough, determined, and he never complained. It is a privilege to be here with him. Watching him has given all of us a new insight on complaining—we won't be doing any! If he can make it with his challenges, who are we to do any less?" —David

Day 4: Tuesday, July 3

"Today was both easy and hard. The easy thing was we really didn't go uphill that much. The hard thing was it was really hot. A park ranger told us it's 115 degrees in Death Valley, which is 76 miles east of here. You know what? Mt. Whitney is the highest place in the USA, and Death Valley is the lowest place. And they're both close to each other. Pretty cool, huh? A marmot almost stole our food today, but we stopped him." —Patrick

"Each night, we put our food in bear boxes and put the boxes up under boulders. Then, we hike and camp away from them. That way, if the bears are attracted to the food, they won't be near us. Today, I asked Patrick what he was trained to do if we saw bears. He said he was told by his dad that he did not have to run faster than the bear; he only had to run faster than Grandpa! David's sense of humor really has been helpful on this trip!" —Doug

"We ran into two park rangers today. One was especially happy to see Patrick. She said she usually goes the whole summer without seeing anyone his age. She emphasized how important it was for this generation to learn to appreciate nature and our national parks system." —David

Day 5: Wednesday, July 4

"Today, we passed Guitar Lake and Timberline Lake. Past Timberline, because of the elevation, no vegetation grows. There simply is not enough oxygen to sustain life. It's all granite from here. At Guitar Lake, we had a full view of Mt. Whitney. It was pretty imposing. Straight plates of granite jutting up into the sky! Water has gotten pretty scarce. One ranger we saw said this is the driest it has been in the 17 years he's been stationed here. We're all so tired. Because of that and in an effort to conserve water, we're not even using our plates and cups anymore. We're just eating 'family style' out of the same pan using our spoons. We're going to sleep out under the stars tonight. The stars are so big, bright and beautiful. The northern star looks like someone's spotlight! And the moon is lighting up the granite on Mt. Whitney like it's daylight. God's amazing creation!" —David

"Today we saw a marmot that seemed like it was posing for us! We took a lot of pictures. We saw a snake with a mouse in its mouth. They were fighting and fell in a stream together. That was funny! Dad keeps calling Uncle Doug 'Bobby Boucher' from the movie 'Waterboy,' because he's the one who keeps pumping the water for us! He does a good job!" —Patrick

"Under the 'best case scenario,' we were supposed to make the summit today. Our hiking conditions, however, have dictated a more staged approach; so, tomorrow will be 'summit day.' I'm glad we planned for an extra day or two. Everyone is tired of the 'beef stick,' me included. We are rationing our 'good' food and planning our strategy to get to the summit. Our wives were expecting us to call today from the summit since that may be the only place in five days for cell phone service. I hope they don't worry about us. We all appreciate their sacrifices in allowing us to be here." —Don Jr.

Day 6: Thursday, July 5

"We started early, at 5:50 this morning and reached the Trail Crest (13,650 feet) at 10:10. Trail Crest is where the trails from the west and east sides meet. We dropped our packs there and made the climb to the peak. The trail was pretty treacherous. Numerous rockslides covered the trail, which was extremely narrow, with 2,500-foot drops on the side. If we had slipped, we would have been goners! At 12:20 p.m., we reached the top where there is a stone house (no one lives there!) and a register log. We all signed our names and had the opportunity to write a comment. I wrote, 'God created the earth.' Patrick wrote, 'It was a great experience, and I loved it!' David wrote, 'I hiked this mountain with my hero [Patrick].' I thanked God for allowing us to reach this moment. We headed back down at 3:15 p.m. to a place on the east side called base camp. We got to base camp at 7:30. I was so exhausted; I just climbed into the tent and fell asleep with no supper." —Don Sr.

"The climb to the top was treacherous. Rockslides made the trails very difficult. The 2,500-foot drop offs were intimidating. The Empire State Building is about 1,500 feet tall. It would be like falling off almost two Empire State Buildings if we slipped. A couple times, I grabbed Patrick's pack to steady him. I figured if he was going to fall, I might as well go with him. I certainly can't go back to Susan without him!" —David

"Oh yeah, I did it! Three generations, baby, on top of that mountain! Here's some advice for people climbing to the top of Mt. Whitney: Don't look down! Number one: You have to stay hydrated. You need water. It's your friend!" —Patrick

"The image of Grandpa and Patrick walking to the summit together will forever be etched in my memory." —Doug

"At the top of the mountain, I overheard Patrick say to his Dad, 'Maybe someday I can bring my son here, and we can hike this mountain with you.' That was priceless. And that's what it's all about. (And David's response was, 'It doesn't necessarily need to be *this* mountain!')" —Don Jr.

"We ran out of water today. We knew it was a risk. But a miracle happened on the way to the summit. A young man met us and hiked to the summit with us. His name was Gary, from Wisconsin. I thought it was strange that he was hiking with a staff. Most hikers use steel walking poles. He said he was hiking the Pacific Coast Trail, from Mexico to Canada. That really put things in perspective! Anyway, after we summited, he said, 'Here, you're going to need this,' and he handed Don a bottle of water! It didn't make sense to me . . . no one carries *bottled* water; everybody filters water from the streams. And the bottle was sealed, so he definitely didn't filter it. There is *nowhere* around here to buy water, either. When we looked back to talk to him, he was gone. And when we made it back to our packs at the Trail Crest, there was another bottle of water there! The Lord took care of us!!" —David

"It's difficult to put into words the overwhelming joy I felt on top of Mt. Whitney with my son. He is STRONG. He faced his fears and overcame the altitude and discomfort. His attitude has been great. He's been all about just getting the job done, but he has taken the time to appreciate the scenery and his family along the way. I think Patrick has realized for the first time that in a man's world, he belongs. This hike has given me a great opportunity to reflect on family. Everyone had something they brought to the family team: Don Jr. brought his hiking expertise, Doug brought his sheer physical strength and water pumping skills, and Dad and Patrick motivated and inspired us. We, like all families, have individuals who are strong in some areas and challenged in others.

One person's challenge is compensated by another person's strength. The goal was—and always is—to *finish together!*" —David

Day 7: Friday, July 6

"Well, I've come to find out Patrick will allow himself to starve rather than eat something he doesn't like! He had his fill of the trail food we brought, and as of this morning, he hadn't eaten in 24 hours. For that reason, we all decided to allow me and Patrick to go ahead down the trail to a place called the Portal, the finish line so to speak. All I had to mention was the hamburger, and Patrick was off and running! Dad, Don, and Doug finished about 2 hours later and joined Patrick in eating hamburgers. Yes, Patrick ate a second round with them!" —David

"Today was a difficult day—6 miles downhill and an elevation drop of 5,500 feet, and my knees were already shot. I was using my poles defensively. At one point, we met three hikers heading up the trail. They said they had met David and Patrick and that they had made it and called our wives. That was good news. We wished them well and moved on. I didn't go 20 steps before this wave of weakness swept over my body, my knees gave way, and I went down. Don Jr. yelled for the three hikers to come help. Everyone was buzzing around me. Don Jr. was checking my blood sugar; it was okay. Doug said, 'Give me that pack,' and then he strapped it to his pack and headed downhill as fast as he could go to get help. The hikers said something about my electrolytes being off, and gave me a Gatorade to drink. I felt better in a few minutes and was able to stand up again. The hikers had started on their way again, when suddenly, they turned back and said, 'We would like to pray for you.' They laid their hands on me and prayed. I felt a renewed strength after that. I know many people have been praying for us during this trip, and it means so much to me. Finally, we made it to the end of the trail. (Doug met us halfway with more Gatorade.) I wore a pedometer the whole time we hiked. At the end, it said I had taken 89,000 steps!" —Don Sr.

"Close to the end of the trail, we passed an Asian family, and the mother said to her husband and two children, 'Those are *real* hikers.' She was talking about me and Dad! It made me feel proud.

Lots of people congratulated us at the end. They made a big fuss that I was only 14 and had made that hike. Dad told me most people who hike this mountain are between the ages of 25 and 30. It makes me feel good that I did it!" —Patrick

"Patrick was a joy and inspiration. He was amazing. He had to attack situations that most teenagers and young adults would have passed on . . . altitude, fatigue, sleeping in 'not so comfortable' conditions, eating 'poor' food (I suppose he won't want lasagna for a long time after he gets home), heat, lack of cold water, having to carry 'that stupid pack,' not to mention hiking a peak that the vast majority of people would not even consider attempting. The growth I saw in Patrick during our week's hike was incredible." — Doug

"That hamburger was the best hamburger I've had in my whole life! It was really great to hike with my dad, grandpa, and uncles. I had not been with my uncles in a really long time since they live in California. I love my family. That's what God wants all of us to do—love our families." —Patrick

"This trip was not so much about the struggles, or even about getting to the top of the mountain. It was about the journey. About the initiation into manhood. About the honoring of a father, and about three brothers affirming their love for each other. It was about the Lord meeting us at every turn in the trail." — David

***

It was great to get my hikers home. My brother-in-law Don Jr. kept saying about the hike as they planned it, "You can't out-dream God." He was right. Something happened on those trails that I can't explain. Patrick had this new confidence, a greater sense of self-assurance. He was holding his head a little higher, and his step was a little brighter. As my father-in-law said as we left the airport upon their return, "He left a boy and came home a man."

I learned from the Mt. Whitney experience that the Lord sometimes asks us to go into scary, intimidating places . . . but He doesn't have us go there alone. He is with us, and He has lessons for us during that journey, lessons that can only be learned in that scary, intimidating place. David's call to say they had completed the hike came two days after it was due. I had to fight panic, remembering the Lord was over this trip. I had to trust Him over and over. I prayed, and He kept reassuring me that everything was okay, that I needed to wait. And then David called!

"Honey, we made it!" he shouted.

I cheered and jumped for joy right on the sidewalk where I was standing. What an accomplishment! And when I saw Patrick, and the other men, after the trip, I knew the Lord had touched all their lives with His power, love, care, and wisdom during a trip that would mold their lives forever. We did not have to fear because the Lord was with all of us. We did not need to be dismayed, because He is our God. He did strengthen us and help us; He held all of us up with His righteous right hand. Just like He said on that tattered scrap of paper with the words from Isaiah 41:10.

And during the process, a father taught his son about being a man. Patrick learned to be strong by facing his fears and trusting in God. He saw "the men of the family" work together and take care of one another. He viewed their personal strengths, their commitment to family, and their dedication to the Lord. He spent valuable time with male role models whom he admired. His Father in heaven and his father on earth had taught him some valuable lessons which would impact him for years to come.

Patrick's Perspective:

I am grateful to have had that trip with the King men. I admire and respect each one of them. At first, I did not want to take the trip because I was paralyzed with fear. I finally did it because God reassured me that I needed to do it. God helped Dad, his brothers, Grandpa, and me during the whole trip. That mountain was beautiful. Pictures could never do it justice. God made an amazing world! I feel like I am a stronger person because of that trip. When hard things come in my life, I can always look back and say, "Well, I hiked Mount Whitney!"

SOMETHING TO THINK ABOUT:

How could you "release" someone you love

to be taught by another?

Who might serve as a good role model

for you or someone you love?

What experiences or activities might place you or

someone you love in a position to be influenced

by positive role models?

Would you seek the Lord about how He would like you to

grow personally, and who might help you to do so?

David and Patrick standing above
an area just hiked

Patrick and David on top of Mt. Whitney

*Don Sr., Don Jr., Patrick, and David making
their descent from the top of the mountain*

*Patrick, David, Don. Sr., Doug, and Don Jr.
at the completion of their 7-day hike*

*Patrick enjoying the long-anticipated hamburger
with his dad, grandpa, and uncle*

13

REALIZING GOD WORKS WONDERS

"Who is like You among the gods, O Lord?
Who is like You, majestic in holiness,
awesome in praises, working wonders?"
—*Exodus 15:11, NASB*

Patrick tentatively placed one foot in front of the other as he carefully scaled the steps in front of him.

A knot twisted its way in my stomach.

What have I done? I thought, feeling a sense of panic starting to squeeze me in its vise.

What if they don't receive him well?

What if he forgets the words and panics?

Having completed his ascent, Patrick slowly turned around and smiled at the sanctuary full of people. Rapidly becoming his signature trademark, his smile washed over the assembly of people like a wave of sweetness, acceptance, and love.

The notes of his music track began to drift through the sound system.

Dear Lord, please help him! And bless the people here with his song, Your song, I prayed.

About six months ago, Patrick had said, "Do you think I could sing in church?"

The idea startled me.

"Why do you want to sing in church?" I asked.

"Because my chorus teacher said I have a gift, and I should

sing in church. I have been praying about it, and I think God wants me to do it."

Well, that settled it. When God told Patrick to do something, he was going to do it. He didn't waver. When God tells you to do something, you do it, according to Patrick. That's it.

"What do you want to sing?" I asked.

"'Give Me Jesus.' The one sung by Fernando Ortega.[viii] You know, I sang it for my performance piece in chorus this year," Patrick said.

I looked into his eyes, one sparkling blue and the other a deep-set green, and I knew he was determined to move forward with his plans.

"Okay. Let's talk to Russ and Debbie (our music minister and his assistant) about it," I said, wondering where the Lord was going with all this.

Patrick was 16 and had never sung in church. I was just grateful he could handle being in the school chorus, navigating all the melodies and movements that were part of that program.

My mind travelled back a few years to when Patrick had randomly been assigned to an exploratory chorus class at school. As a sixth grader at China Grove Middle School, Patrick would arbitrarily be placed in an exploratory class each nine weeks, to "explore" different fields of study in order to discover if those areas interested him.

After about two weeks into chorus, Patrick's teacher Mrs. Morris called me. I braced myself. Calls from teachers usually meant challenges and problems to be addressed.

"Mrs. King?"

"Yes?" I responded.

"I am Mrs. Morris, Patrick's chorus teacher, and I was just wondering if you knew that Patrick has a gift in singing."

Shock replaced fear.

"What?!" I asked, not certain I had heard her correctly.

"Patrick has a gift in singing," she repeated. "Have you heard him sing?"

"No," I replied.

Patrick would always retreat to his bedroom to practice his chorus material. Located in the basement, far away from noise and other sensory intrusions, Patrick's bedroom served as a refuge from the world, where he could decompress and retrain his focus on important matters. When he chose to concentrate on his singing, I barely heard a sound, other than an occasional stray note that worked its way up through the floorboards to the first floor.

"Well, I think he may have perfect pitch," Mrs. Morris said. "His ear hears the music perfectly, and he is able to reproduce it exactly as he hears it. Your son has a gift," she declared for the third time. "I just thought you ought to know."

I was amazed. Patrick couldn't talk for the longest time, and now I was being told he could sing, and not just sing but sing well. From that point forward, music interwove itself into Patrick's life like a golden thread in a tapestry. He embraced music, and music embraced him. His face softened when he sang, and the day's problems melted and were swept away into the pulsating current of melodies, harmonies, and rhythms. Music became a refuge for Patrick.

"I can feel God when I sing," Patrick said.

The rising music brought me back to the sanctuary. *Oh, Lord! Here we go!* I thought.

The sound of his singing brought a hush over the congregation.

A beauty swept through the room. The power and magnificence of truth wrapped in glorious music. I was watching a miracle unfold. Tears of joy cascaded down my cheeks. I could feel the truth behind Patrick's song. I could feel Jesus' presence with all of us. I looked around and realized others were feeling Him too, as many tears flowed and people began wiping their eyes and focusing on the young man before them.

Patrick sang with a pure voice and innocent trust, glorifying Jesus, whom he loved.

The congregation was mesmerized. Finally, the last notes of the song drifted from his mouth and made their ascent toward heaven. Having completed his mission, Patrick smiled one last time and began his slow, awkward descent down the red carpeted steps, training his eyes on each step along the journey.

The crowd sat in silence. Then, a man at the front of the congregation rose to his feet and began clapping loudly for Patrick. One by one, others stood and began applauding, until everyone in the church was giving Patrick a standing ovation!

Joy exploded in my heart.

Look at what You did, Lord! I rejoiced.

About halfway down the steps, Patrick looked up in response to the commotion. Shock registered on his face.

He stopped, uncertain of what to do. Then he smiled again, nodded, and slowly worked his way down the rest of the stairs.

Immediately, I went back in time again.

September 28, 1996. I was at the Billy Graham Crusade in Charlotte, North Carolina. Life had become overwhelming, and I was at the breaking point. I could no longer juggle the mounting demands of home, work, and family.

Michael W. Smith was singing. Then Billy Graham got up to speak. I didn't hear a word he was saying. That's because the Lord was speaking to me the entire time. I could feel it in my heart. Essentially, He was telling me, "Susan, you've come to Me over and over again with little pieces of your life that you wanted Me to fix. Now it's time for you to give Me your entire life."

So when they gave the invitation, I knew I was supposed to go down onto the field of the Charlotte Panthers Stadium and do just that. The problem was that fear immediately set in. I didn't know how this whole thing worked—what was I supposed to do, what was I supposed to say? And what about the people I came with? Would they think I was crazy?

Lord, I prayed, *I know You want me to go down there. Please help me get up and out of my seat.*

Immediately, my daughter Katie leaped out of her seat. Still the passionate one in our family, Katie was nine years old at the time. She had accompanied me and David to the crusade on a travel bus our church had rented.

"Come on, Mom, let's go!" she pressed.

"Katie!" David said. "Do you know why people are going down there?"

"No, I don't," she announced. "I just know that Mom and I are supposed to go."

No obstacle was going to stop that child. She led me between the metal bars that separated the different sections of the stadium, over the folding chairs that lined the many rows in the arena, and into the teeming crowd that was filling the artificial turf. Then she stopped, looking around expectantly.

A gentleman approached me and said, "Would you like to accept Jesus into your heart?" and I heard myself say, "Yes."

"Wait right here, and we will find someone to talk with you," he said.

But I was moving, being ushered along again by my determined daughter.

A lady about my age approached and began talking with us. I hung on her every word. First, because I wanted to know how to give my life to Jesus. I was ready to do that. But I also had to listen ever so carefully to her because she had a speech impediment. She produced sounds with much effort, like she was giving birth to the words, and I strained to understand her expressions. Actually, I was grateful, because her speech difficulties were making me focus intently on each word, and I did not want to miss one of them.

She told me how much God loved each one of us, how much He loved me and Katie. She said God's plan, as outlined in the Bible, has always been for mankind to have peace and life in Him. But then she explained how man chose to sin, or to go our own way apart from God. She said sin began with Adam and Eve and has been passed down in our nature ever since.

Then, she showed me a picture. It had a man standing on one side of a mountain that was broken in half. The man was positioned on the left side, which was labeled "People," and a huge chasm existed between that side and the right side, which was labeled "God." She wrote the word "sin" in the middle of the chasm and told me, "Sin is what separates us from God, and we can't do anything to fix that problem. We try to get across that chasm through good works, religion, morality, and various philosophies about life, but they don't work."

Then she drew a huge cross vertically through the word "sin," and she explained, "Only God could take care of the sin problem, and He did it through Jesus."

She drew the horizontal beam of the cross from the left side of the mountain, across the vertical beam of the cross, and over to the right side of the mountain where "God" was. She looked at me and said, "Jesus is the way to solve this separation between us and God. When He died on the cross and rose again from the grave, He paid the penalty for our sin and bridged the gap between us and God. His death and resurrection make a new life possible for everyone who believes in Him. Will you choose to believe in Him today?"

"Yes!" Katie and I answered in unison. We looked at each

other, delighted, and smiled.

Then that wonderful woman with the cleft palate led me and Katie in praying to receive Jesus into our hearts. We admitted our sin, put our faith in what Jesus did to pay for our sin, and announced that we wanted to live our lives for Him and with Him from that point forward.

A few months later, I was making my bed in the morning, and I stopped, halted by a thought that had just entered my mind.

Lord, I prayed. *I know nothing happens by accident in Your economy. I was just wondering . . . was there a reason why You had a handicapped person lead me to Christ?*

I sensed His answer immediately.

"It's because of your son," He whispered. "I can use anyone I want to."

At that time, Patrick was 3, and he was floundering in a world of chaos, unable to speak or to relate to the discordant world around him.

I pondered the Lord's words in my heart for many years to come. Now, 13 years later, they were returning to me.

Now, at First Baptist Church in Salisbury, the words had come alive before my eyes. Here was my son, the boy who couldn't talk, and he was *singing*! His song had risen from the depths of his heart, where Jesus lived. God had just used him to touch the lives of hundreds of people in our church.

From there, Patrick went on to sing in his school choruses until he graduated from high school. He was chosen for the North Carolina State Honors Chorus twice while in high school, and he sang on the stage at Carnegie Hall in New York City as part of the National Youth Choir. His singing continues to touch hearts and amaze those around him.

Patrick's Perspective:

I have felt very close to God through my autism and my life's struggles. I am glad He has given me the gift of singing because I feel His closeness when I sing. God says He "is able to do far more abundantly than all that we ask or think, according to the power at work within us" (Ephesians 3:20, ESV). I could not talk when I was younger. Now, I not only talk, but I can also sing! God did that, and I consider it a miracle. I am very happy when I get to sing about how wonderful God is and the great things He has done. I am glad when other people tell me that my singing makes them feel closer to God.

Since I was young, God taught me that He loves me. So many people in my life have taken the time to encourage me and talk to me. God has given me a huge "family" in the world. I feel loved and accepted by the people in my life for who I am, even though I am different. And because others love and accept me, I came to understand that God does too.

At age 8, I understood that Jesus died on the cross for me because He loved me and wanted to save me from my sins, and I accepted Him as my Lord and Savior. I got baptized that year. I had to stand on a plastic box to get baptized because I was so small. Becoming a Christian changed my whole life! I want you to know that being kind, smiling, and talking to a child or young person does make a difference. It is hard being a teenager sometimes—especially a teenager with autism—but the kindness of others makes it a lot easier.

I am overwhelmed that God sent His only Son to die for me on the cross, and because of that, I can have a great life here, and I get to be with Him forever. Because of Jesus, He has already shown me how much He loves me, so I can trust Him today and every day.

SOMETHING TO THINK ABOUT:

Do you believe God can work wonders?

Do you believe God can work His wonders through you?

Can you see that the greatest wonder worked by God is

Jesus' death and resurrection on your behalf?

Does Jesus live in your heart? . . . completely?

If you do not know Jesus as your personal Lord and Savior,

consider praying this prayer, today:

Jesus, thank You for dying on the cross to pay the penalty for my sins

and to make a way to God the Father. I know I haven't always lived as

I should. I thank You for forgiving me and taking my sins away. I

believe in what You accomplished for me in Your death and resurrection.

I believe in You. And I want to live the rest of my life with You and for

You. Come into my heart and stay there forever. Amen.

If you prayed that prayer, please tell someone at your

local church, so they can help you continue growing in

your relationship with the Lord.

Patrick's baptism

*Patrick and his parents in New York City, where he
sang with the National Youth Choir at Carnegie Hall*

14

SPEAKING LIFE OVER OTHERS

"Death and life are in the power of the tongue."
—Proverbs 18:21, NASB

"**I** don't understand why Patrick didn't get an A on his test," I told David in frustration. Dishes scraped and glasses clanked as we ran them under the steady stream of water at the sink and loaded the dishwasher after dinner.

"How did the studying go?" David asked.

"That's just it. He knew the material. He knew it all. He asked me to quiz him, and he could answer every question," I said with a sigh.

I remembered the "cord in the outlet" example from the TEACCH Center. Sue McCarter had told me autistic people were like cords plugged into the electrical socket. Sometimes, the connection was good, and the cord and the socket were firmly connected. Other times, the cord hung out of the socket, with the prongs barely making contact with the power source inside the outlet. On those days, the autistic individual feels disconnected, unable to function at previous levels.

I wondered if Patrick had experienced one of those days when he took his test.

A "C" wasn't the end of the world, but I knew Patrick had worked hard. In my mind, he should have done better.

Later that night, Patrick timidly approached me and asked, "Can I talk to you?"

"Of course," I said, swiveling around in the chair at my desk. "Let's go sit on the couch."

We each took positions across from one another on the comfy cushions.

"Are you disappointed in me?" Patrick stammered, lowering his head.

I felt the sense of shock bring my mind to full attention.

"No! Of course not!" I said, wondering what this was all about.

"I heard you and Dad talking in the kitchen," Patrick added, refusing to raise his eyes to mine.

Oh no, I thought, alarm rising. I had forgotten about Patrick's hearing.

We had discovered that Patrick possessed hyper-sensitive hearing. Often, autistic individuals command extremely strong abilities in some areas. For Patrick, his hearing excelled beyond the norm.

One day, when we were coming down the stairs from the second to the first floor in our home, Patrick announced, "The TV is on."

"No, it's not," I said.

"I will show you," Patrick said. He walked me over to the TV set and promptly pointed to the power button, which was glowing a bright green.

"I can hear it," he said matter-of-factly.

"You can hear that?" I asked, just to make sure I had understood him correctly.

"Yes. I can hear it. And I can hear the electricity humming in the walls, too," he added.

"What do you mean?" I asked.

He took my hand and led me over to the wall and pointed to an electrical outlet.

"Right there," he said.

. . . I had forgotten about Patrick's hearing. When David and I were discussing Patrick's test, Patrick had been in another part of the house, two rooms away, but distance doesn't matter when you have that kind of hearing. It suddenly dawned on me that Patrick had heard every word.

"We are never disappointed in you, Patrick," I said.

"You said I should have gotten an A," he said.

"Patrick, Dad and I will always be proud of you, especially when you try hard and do your best," I said, hoping he would believe those words.

He looked up at me.

"Did you do your best?" I asked.

"Yes," he said. "I just had trouble remembering some of the stuff. I don't know why."

"Well, then, that's great!" I said. "I am so proud of you!"

His eyes widened in surprise.

"Can I give you a hug?" I asked, with a lilt in my voice.

"Okay," Patrick said.

I hugged him tightly and whispered in his ear, "You are doing great, Patrick. And I admire you for how hard you are trying at school."

His characteristic smile began to work its way across his face.

Even though we had this sweet interchange, the "quest for A's" became Patrick's focus for many years to come. Based on my words, he had created a new rule in his mind that good students get A's, and he wanted desperately to be a good student.

The entire interchange made me stop and think. From that point forward, I tried to frame my words as if Patrick were listening. (Most of the time, he probably was!) I intentionally drew out encouraging words, hope-filled words, words of faith from the library in my mind. Then, I took it even further. When I was speaking about anyone, I tried to choose my words as if they were in the next room listening.

One day, as I was thinking about this perspective, I realized that the Lord hears everything I say, whether I speak the words with my mouth or in my mind. He hears it all. I began choosing my words based on the truth that He was listening. I certainly have not mastered this approach, but it has helped me understand the power of my words. "Death and life are in the power of the tongue," according to Proverbs 18:21, NASB. I want my tongue to speak life to those around me. I want my words to build people up and to show them God's grace as it says in Ephesians 4:29, NASB: "Let no unwholesome word proceed from your mouth, but only such a word as is good for edification, according to the need of the moment, so that it will give grace to those who hear." I try to ask myself when I am tempted to say something: *Is it necessary? Will what*

I want to say build up someone? Will what I want to say show someone the grace of God?

Patrick and I have experienced a lot of "building up" and an abundance of God's grace through his many teachers over the years. An overwhelming majority of the teachers, counselors, and administrators who worked with Patrick chose to speak life into his soul. They chose to see potential in him and voiced words of affirmation and encouragement so that he bloomed like a seed in the fertile soil of hope.

His first teacher was Mrs. Grey Calvert. She took Patrick under her wing when he was 5 and supposed to enter kindergarten. Due to the Preschool Outreach Program, Patrick was identified as a student who could use some extra help before he ventured into the world of kindergarten, so he was recommended to attend Mrs. Calvert's transitional class. The entire focus of this classroom was to help Patrick make the transition to kindergarten within a year.

Located at Isenberg Elementary School in Salisbury, the transitional classroom held out the hope of someday attending "regular school." But its greatest prospect for possibilities was Mrs. Calvert. She fiercely believed in her students' ability to make progress, and she told them so with her words and expectations.

"You can do this, Patrick!" she told him whenever he balked at a new challenge or routine. I rejoiced to find an ally in Patrick's teacher, but she challenged me, too. "You have to back up these things at home, Mom," she said, referring to the academic and behavioral expectations, practices, and structures. "What's cute at 5 is a curse at 15." I never forgot those words. She saw a *future* for my son, and she wanted him to be well prepared for it. I couldn't thank God for her enough. With Mrs. Calvert, Patrick tackled numbers and letters, shapes, and colors. With her, he learned how to walk in a line to the cafeteria, how to sit at a desk to do his work, and how to participate in the other numerous routines required in a school environment.

At the end of the year, I took Patrick to a DIAL Screening for kindergarten. It involved a series of tests to check his competency in a variety of areas, with the ultimate goal of determining his readiness for kindergarten. I walked him into the media center at China Grove Elementary School, where the testing would take place. I immediately flashed back to lots of former tests where we heard words like "mentally retarded," "slow," and "inadequate."

Oh Lord, help Patrick to enjoy this experience. Help him to do his best. Please incline these teachers to be kind to him and patient with him, I prayed.

"Is this Patrick?" a friendly blonde lady asked.

"Yes," I answered.

"We are so glad you are here today, Patrick," she said. "We are going to go play some games together, right over there. Is that okay?"

Patrick nodded shyly, and off they went.

I kept up my prayer vigil.

About 30 minutes later, the same friendly blonde returned.

"Mrs. King, can you come with me?" she asked.

I followed her over to a small side room where Patrick was waiting.

"I would like to go over the results of Patrick's screening," she said with a big smile. "Your son has scored in the 95th percentile, which means only 5 percent of the students taking these tests have results higher than his. He is definitely ready for kindergarten!"

My heart leaped with joy! The news caught me completely off guard.

"Wow! Oh, I'm so happy! Thank you! Thank you!"

I couldn't find the right words to express the depth of my gratitude, the height of my happiness. I could not wait to tell Mrs. Calvert. I drove straight to Isenberg and made a beeline for her.

"He blew the numbers off the chart, didn't he?" she asked before I could say a word.

Tears found their way out of my grateful heart and down my cheeks.

"Yes," I said, nodding my head.

"I knew he would," she said.

"Thank you for everything you have done to help him," I said. "You have made such a difference in his life."

"Patrick did all the work," she said.

I knew better.

Through the years, the Lord brought a steady stream of kind and wise teachers into Patrick's life. I remember Becky Daniel, his kindergarten teacher, who eagerly embraced what she called Patrick's "quirkiness" and further helped him adjust to the world of school. At the time, Patrick was obsessed with the Veggie Tales character named "Larry Boy," and Mrs. Daniel incorporated Larry

Boy into her classroom and teaching in order to keep Patrick's attention.

I remember Sue Dodd, who went to the principal and fought to have Patrick in her fifth grade classroom because she wanted to help him get grounded and strong before he entered middle school. She taught Patrick about getting along with others through "family meetings" with the students in her class. She wiped away tears on the day she had to say goodbye and send him on to middle school.

And I remember Jan Gore, Patrick's chorus teacher in high school, who met with me and Patrick before he entered South Rowan High School and talked with us about how we could help Patrick when he became stressed and overwhelmed. She shaped the chorus into a family where Patrick belonged.

Over time, I found it helped to communicate with Patrick's teachers so they could better understand him. Whenever Patrick was about to have a new group of teachers, I would request a meeting with them. I wanted them to get to know Patrick ahead of time. I always took a list of his "strengths" and "challenges" as well as a list of "suggestions," which included approaches that might help him in the classroom.

During our meeting, I shared stories from Patrick's life that emphasized my points. The teachers especially liked the stories and would laugh and smile in response. It warmed my heart to see their openness and willingness to embrace my son and all the traits that make him unique. Once, when I walked into one of those meetings, a veteran teacher told me, "I have been researching on the Internet about autism so I could learn more about it and find out how to best serve your son." In his later years in high school, Patrick would go over the list of strengths, challenges, and suggestions with his new teachers himself. He was learning to advocate for himself in anticipation of college.

Some of the items on Patrick's "strengths" list included:

Well-mannered
Desire to do well in school
Desire to learn best behaviors
Creative
Cares about other people
Appreciative

Sincere/honest
Good memorization skills
A/B student
Good sense of humor
Teachable/continues to progress
Happy, well-adjusted, pleasant
Wants to please his teachers
Detail-oriented
Likes and follows routines
Computer skills
Enjoys school/learning
Strong desire to succeed

His list of challenges included:

Socialization
Over-obsession on certain topics/conversation
Literalness in conversation/reading
Hypersensitivity to sound, smell, pain
Can get over-stimulated by too much sensory stimulation—need to withdraw
Note-taking
Doesn't always understand instructions
Test anxiety (wants all A's)
Multi-tasking
"Letting go" of concerns

Suggestions to help Patrick have included:

1. Tell him what you are going to do before you do it; advise him beforehand if possible of "sensory invasions."
2. Make sure he understands instructions/expectations (repeat back to you?).
3. Advise him on the "social rules" if you see he needs help.
4. Redirect him if he over-obsesses.
5. Use sticky notes on his desk for focus: "Let it go," "don't talk," etc.
6. Try to be literal in instructions/conversations, or explain meanings of word plays, etc. Tell him if you are teasing or being sarcastic.

7. Seat him toward the front of the class to minimize distractions.
8. Pair him with a responsible, understanding student.
9. Let him take a break/withdraw/take a "time out" if he gets overloaded.
10. Have him look at you when you are giving instructions.
11. Provide written copies of notes (to check his notes against).
12. Try to avoid long strings of directions.
13. Use a calm voice when dealing with him.
14. Encourage him to use his skills, strengths in school, to help other students.
15. Allow him to take tests in sections or take tests home.
16. Maintain routines.
17. Let him know he's doing okay.

Patrick's teachers and I would have other meetings, too, when specific issues arose, and we would problem solve together. I will never forget Patrick's sixth-grade year when his team of teachers called me and requested a meeting. When we met, I was told that Patrick kept disrupting the class, speaking out, telling jokes, and making noises. They wanted to know if I had any idea about what might be prompting this behavior and if I had any suggestions for dealing with it.

"Let me talk with Patrick and try to find out about it," I said.

"It's Dad's fault," Patrick said, when I asked him about it.

Dumbfounded, I said, "What! Why is it Dad's fault?"

Patrick explained, "Because Dad is funny, and he has a lot of friends. I thought if I could be funny, then I would have a lot of friends, too."

I felt such empathy. Middle school memories flooded in. Trying to make friends, trying to fit in, trying to find your place in the sea of other students who also were thrashing and grasping for identity.

"Patrick," I said, "What happens when you are trying to be funny? What do the other students do?"

"They look at me, and sometimes they laugh," Patrick said.

"Do you think the teacher can keep teaching if everyone is looking and laughing at you?" I asked. "Do you think the students can learn if you are distracting them?"

I saw the wheels turning in his head.

"I'm sorry! I'm so sorry!" he said, as a panicked expression displayed itself on his face.

"It's okay to be funny," I said, "just not while the teacher is trying to teach. Do you think you can remember that and do it?"

"Yes, I will," Patrick said.

His teachers laughed out loud when I told them Patrick's response, and I thanked God for their sense of humor.

Throughout Patrick's various academic environments, we have had Individual Education Plans, 504 Plans, and numerous meetings and paperwork sessions to maintain them. We've set academic and social goals for Patrick, and we've monitored his progress toward reaching them. One of his academic accommodations involved receiving extended time on tests; another focused on providing testing in a separate room away from the class. These special arrangements allowed Patrick to be free from distractions and to be able to have the extra time necessary to focus his mind and get his fingers to do the required writing.

Over the years, teachers would let him go to the water fountain to take a break when he was feeling overwhelmed. They would use pictures and written notes to remind him to do things. They would pair him with a responsible student who was willing to help Patrick and who felt a reward in doing so. The high school office secretary even let him use the bathroom there because of the "sensory overload" found in the students' bathrooms.

Through my many and varied experiences with the wonderful servants in our public school system, I have developed a deep, unshakable respect for them. Despite the many demands placed on them, the teachers and administrators I have encountered have passionately performed their duties of educating students, developing character, and changing lives as an endless stream of learners came through their doors. I continually asked them what I could do to help them, not only regarding the needs of my child, but also regarding their responsibilities to other students. I have served as a proctor for all sorts of testing, walking through the room and silently praying for the students and their teachers while monitoring their test taking. I have helped to make copies and to chaperone trips and activities. I have made donations of both time and resources. But, most of all, I have tried to encourage these devoted teachers and staff members and to thank them for their priceless gift of investing in the life of my child.

We have driven off the road to academic success and landed in the ditch a few times, but Patrick's teachers have always been there to help lift us back onto the road again. I remember when Patrick went to take his final exam in high school chemistry. After about two hours, Patrick's teacher called me.

"Mrs. King, Patrick had a complete meltdown while trying to take the test," said Mr. Greg Yanz, his chemistry teacher. "He sat there for two hours and only answered one question. He kept saying, 'I can't remember the formulas,' and Mrs. King, they were at the top of the page. I finally realized that he just wasn't going to be able to do it today, so I told him to stop. He is in the guidance office, and he is pretty upset. You need to come get him. I told him he could retake the test on the makeup day for exams, and I would be glad to meet with him before then to help him review. He knows the material. He just needs to be reminded that he knows it."

When Patrick left to take the test that morning, I knew it was going to be rough. The cord was not connected to the socket. Fretting, anxiety, and fearfulness had already started interfering with the ability of his mind to link with the test.

When I got to the guidance office, I found Patrick in the conference room, pacing, sobbing, and talking to himself.

"I failed. I could not remember. What if I fail chemistry? What if I fail high school? Why couldn't I remember?" he kept repeating.

"Patrick," I said firmly. "Look at me."

He stopped his mantra and looked at me.

"It is okay," I said. "You have had a bad day. You can recover from this."

"I couldn't remember," he said, his lower lip trembling.

"I know. Your teacher called me. He is going to let you take the test on makeup day."

"What if I don't remember then?" Patrick said.

"God is going to help you so you can remember," I said. "And He already is sending Mr. Yanz to help you."

"Really?" Patrick asked.

The reality of a God of second chances was settling in.

"Let's go home, where you can relax," I said, "and we will look at chemistry again tomorrow."

Patrick met with his chemistry teacher a few days later and reviewed the material further. On the day of the makeup exam, Patrick went out the door with a big smile on his face. He believed he could do it. Mr. Yanz called me two hours later.

"Mrs. King, Patrick made a 95 on the exam," he said. "Please tell him when he gets home so that he won't have to worry about it. And tell him congratulations. I knew he could do it."

Moments like those rank right up there with the best Christmas ever! To watch your child persevere and succeed because another caring adult has championed his success fills your heart with overflowing gratitude. I could never thank Mr. Yanz or Patrick's other teachers enough.

Due to Patrick's determination and the continued devotion of his teachers, this young man who was diagnosed as "mentally retarded" ended up graduating high school with a 4.125 weighted grade point average! He received significant academic scholarships to attend college. In addition, he completed his freshman year in college with a 3.97 grade point average, earning a perfect 4.0 his second semester!

The Bible says, "Encourage one another day after day, as long as it is still called 'Today'" (Hebrews 3:13, NASB). That's exactly what Patrick's teachers have done for him. Look at what happened as a result! The right words of encouragement can change someone's life. Watching my son bloom under the sunshine of others' encouraging words has given me the desire to do the same for others—to look for and act on opportunities to encourage those around me. Life can be hard. Everyone has burdens, but the weight of those burdens can be lessened when we reach out and encourage one another. I learned that lesson from watching my son.

I wrote and gave the following poem to Patrick's kindergarten teacher Becky Daniel. I would like to dedicate it to all of Patrick's amazing teachers:

You Made a Difference in the Life of This One

When I birthed my fourth child, oh the dreams that I had.
Since he was my first son, "he'll be different," I said.
I was eager to experience what those differences would be.
But as the days passed, "different" changed for me.

My son, he was "special"—not like other boys.
His movements were jerky, his "words" were just noise.
I struggled for wisdom in how to care for this child,
In ways I could reach him, to touch the person inside.

The world all around us wasn't so welcoming anymore.
Many places we went, they would just slam the door.
"This boy is too different," the people would say.
"We don't have the patience for one made this way."

And I'd hold my little boy as our world tossed and turned.
And I'd pray, "Lord, I know he has a place in Your world."
When time for school came, my heart trembled with fear.
"Oh, Lord, please let somebody love my child here."

The first time we met you, I knew you were the one—
Divinely appointed to care for my son.
My child, he was met with a smile from the start,
And as the days passed, you reached into his heart.

With you was acceptance, and safety, a friend—
If the work got too tough, you'd say, "Try! . . . Try again!"
You looked at this boy and saw something inside.
Your love and compassion touched his heart and his mind.

His potential exploded—he could see; he could do!
He felt loved and encouraged when he was with you.
School became a good place inside of his soul—
Because you saw him not as one different, but whole!

My son now is older; more school years have passed.
His improvements are steady; they all seem to last.
You've gotten new students; each year they come.
But always remember: You made a difference in this one!

Patrick's Perspective:

I gave Mrs. Daniel the gold medallion I got for climbing Mt. Whitney. She helped me climb many mountains, and she definitely deserved a medal! All my teachers deserve one. God has put some amazing teachers in my life over the years. Those teachers embraced me and worked with me to help me not only do well in school but also do well in life. I will never forget them. I'm grateful for the kindness and encouragement of my teachers. They have worked with me to help me succeed in their classes, and they have been willing to do things a little differently for me so I could learn, even with my challenges. I feel like my teachers and the people at school are my friends. They always have a smile and an encouraging word for me. I have needed that. I need to be told I can do it, because then I believe I can.

If you are a teacher, I want to thank you from the bottom of my heart, for all the students you have helped. If you are a teacher, God has given you a very special job. You have the chance to change someone's life—to help them believe in themselves, to help them succeed. That is what I have experienced. It is a blessing.

My parents, friends, and other family members have also

been big encouragers. They have loved me and supported me through all the challenges I have experienced. When people speak words of hope and encouragement, it changes your life.

By the way, I really do not mind that I have hyper-sensitive hearing . . . I get a lot of valuable information that way!

SOMETHING TO THINK ABOUT:

How could you speak "life" over someone else?

Whom might the Lord be calling you to encourage today?

The next time you are about to speak about someone,

imagine them standing in the next room listening.

Would you speak your words with that picture in mind?

Patrick in Mrs. Calvert's classroom

Patrick with Mrs. Daniel

Patrick and David displaying their ties
with Patrick's favorite hero Larry Boy

Patrick with Mrs. Gore

Patrick celebrating his high school graduation

Susan and Patrick after his graduation ceremonies

15

REFUSING TO MAKE ASSUMPTIONS
ABOUT PEOPLE

"Man looks at the outward appearance,
but the Lord looks at the heart."
—1 Samuel 16:7, NASB

Patrick's literal approach to life can be amusing . . . and dangerous. One day, I experienced the scary aspect of his autism when I received a call from his middle school assistant principal.

"Mrs. King, Patrick sexually harassed a student at school today. I am calling to tell you that if it happens again, he will be expelled from school," she said.

What? my mind screamed. *He doesn't even know what sex is!*

Before I could respond, she said, "I am putting Patrick on the phone so you can talk to him about it."

The next thing I knew, Patrick was blubbering on the other end of the phone, "I'm sorry. I'm sorry, for whatever I did. I won't do it ever again!"

"Patrick," I said calmly. "Do you know what they are talking about? What happened?"

"No," he said, confused.

"Okay," I said. "This is what I want you to do. Take a deep breath."

I could hear him sucking his lungs full of air.

"Okay, I did it," he said.

"All right. Now, I am going to find out what this is all about, and we will talk about it when you get home. Don't worry about it. It is going to be okay. Tell the assistant principal I want to talk with her after you go back to class."

"Okay, Mom," Patrick said.

I have found that Patrick needed to hear over and over that things were going to be okay. Those words took the edge off his fear and panic. Those words enabled him to relax enough to free his brain to think.

Did I think everything was going to be okay? It did not really matter what I thought. Because the truth is we have always been, we always are, and we always will be in the care of the Lord. That makes everything okay . . . more than okay!

After I talked with the assistant principal, I discovered the students had been taught about human sexuality that morning. I knew the material was coming because I had signed the papers for Patrick to receive the instruction. After the class, on the way to lunch, Patrick informed a young lady in line with him, "I would like to have sex with you and make a baby."

I was horrified when I heard those words, then reason set in.

"Patrick, do you know what sex is?" I asked him that night.

"Well, I know it makes a baby," he said.

"Yes, but do you remember what it is? What they explained in class today?" I prompted.

"No," Patrick looked down, as if he was in trouble for not paying closer attention.

I was angry with myself for even letting him attend that class. I should have taught him about this myself, I thought regrettably.

"Why, then, did you talk about sex in the lunch line?" I asked.

"Well, I know it makes a baby, and I would really like to be a father," Patrick said. "I would like to have a family. I love our family."

"I think it's wonderful that you want to be a father someday," I reassured him. "But do you think you could be a father now?"

He looked up at me inquisitively.

"Do you have a job where you could earn money to buy diapers and baby food?" I asked. "How would you go to school and take care of the baby, too?"

Understanding crept across his face.

"I guess now is not a good time for me to be a father," Patrick said.

"You're right, Patrick. I am proud of you for realizing that," I said. "If you stay close to God, He will let you know when the time is right. And one more thing . . ." As long as I had entered the waters of this delicate subject, I might as well keep going, I thought.

" . . . God says we should not have sex until we get married. He says that because He loves us. His perfect plan involves a mom and a dad in a family together, helping each other and looking to God to raise their children. Do you understand that?"

"Yes, I do," Patrick said. "Thanks, Mom."

I was so angry with that assistant principal for not trying to understand my son, for rapidly depositing him in the "bad boy, behavior problem" pile, for uttering threats when she didn't even know my son and his challenges. When someone is in a wheelchair, you can tell they are a special needs individual. With autism, it often is difficult to see the special need immediately. This can lead to lots of misunderstanding.

I've had people tell me my son needed more discipline, that he was spoiled, that he was a troublemaker. It's difficult when others don't really know and understand your child. And if you're not careful, you can start believing you're a bad parent. This is not true. Any parent who loves and has a desire to help their child *is* a good parent.

I have had to develop a thicker skin when it comes to my son. I have had to do what I know is best for him and not worry about what everyone else thinks. The other blessing is that I have been able to educate others about Patrick's special needs, so that they can help him and be more sensitive to others in the future.

Early on, I did a lot of advocating for Patrick. I had meetings, sent a lot of emails, and made many phone calls to teachers. I'd ask how Patrick was doing and if he had anything major coming up like a project or test. I contacted teachers when something happened at school to upset him, and we would problem solve together. I helped Patrick organize and schedule his work, so he could complete it. Later, Patrick learned to do a lot of that for himself, becoming his own advocate.

I admire Patrick because he is not afraid to ask for help. I think it's important to support teachers with lots of positive feedback, also. They need to know how they're helping a special needs child and what a difference they are making in that child's life. Teachers need encouragement, too.

But I definitely have not always done things right.

After my issue with the assistant principal, I wanted to call her, to try to make her more aware of Patrick and other autistic children. I wanted her to value and appreciate him and his sincerity, his gentle heart, his desire to do the right thing and to treat others kindly.

But I didn't.

I felt intimidated by her abruptness and snap judgments.

I left it alone.

However, I did learn an extremely valuable lesson from that experience: Don't be so quick to judge others and pass sentence on them. Don't assume you know why people do the things they do. I have told myself these words in the many years since our middle school encounter. Only God truly sees people's hearts. I can ask Him to help me understand people better, and I can try to gather more information by asking them and others questions about their situation. But I always, always need to be cautious about classifying and categorizing people too quickly.

It says in the Bible, "There is one lawgiver and judge who is able to save and to destroy. But who are you to judge your neighbor?" (James 4:12, HCSB). That scripture tells me to be wise and discerning, but not to set myself up as the judge, hold a trial in my mind, and condemn someone by passing a harsh sentence on them. I am not qualified to be the judge of the universe. Only God is.

Patrick's Perspective:

It is easy to be misunderstood as an autistic person, since we are so literal about things. I never want to do anything to hurt someone's feelings, but sometimes, my literal interpretation of things causes confusion or misunderstanding. One time, my mom asked me who I was playing with at school, and I pointed to a boy nearby and said, "that fat boy." Mom quickly took me aside and explained that calling someone fat hurts their feelings. I did not understand because the boy was fat. Forgive me, whoever that was! Lots of autistic people don't know these underlying social rules like others do. We do not mean to hurt anyone's feelings. We just see the world in more black and white terms, no shades of gray. It is either one way, or it is not.

I also try to look beyond people's outward behaviors and appearances because of my own personal experiences in this regard. One year, in high school chorus, we had a member who had trouble entering conversations with the other chorus members. He did it rather abruptly, often changing the subject. It annoyed the other chorus members, and they started talking about him behind his back. I would not participate in those conversations, and I would try to get them to see his positive qualities. *That boy eventually became a wonderful friend of mine and still is. I always like to emphasize the good traits people have. Everybody should be given a chance to be understood. One of my teammates on my college swim team told me, "You are the nicest person I have ever met." That meant a lot to me.*

SOMETHING TO THINK ABOUT:

Have you made some rash

judgments about someone?

Would you ask the Lord to help you

see that person as He sees them?

Would you think about giving

someone a second chance?

Patrick with Emily, Sarah, Katie, and his parents
during his middle school years
(Photo by Karen Goforth)

16

LEARNING TO FORGIVE

"And forgive us our debts,
as we also have forgiven our debtors."
—*Matthew 6:12, NASB*

I have many memories I revisit. Should I have done something differently for my son in various situations—like the sexual harassment episode? I don't know. I certainly cannot do everything perfectly for my son. That's where grace comes in. God can even make something out of my uncertainties and mistakes. I can forgive myself, and I can choose to forgive others.

I forgave that assistant principal. I forgave myself.

The Lord tells us to "Bear with each other and forgive whatever grievances you may have against one another. Forgive as the Lord forgave you" (Col. 3:13, NIV). If the Lord could forgive me for all my wrongdoings, then I could certainly forgive someone else. Forgiveness does not mean that what happened was okay. It just means that I am giving the whole thing to God, for Him to make sense of it and to handle it. In the Bible, to "forgive" actually translates "to send away." It creates the image of not holding things against people (or ourselves) where they can fester and create bitterness. It means releasing them to God because He loves us and because He tells us to.

At an early age, Patrick took to heart that verse (Col. 3:13) about forgiveness. We taught it to our children, along with other scriptures. Those words became part of Patrick's rules for life. I was immensely grateful Patrick had stored that truth in his heart, especially on one particular day when I needed his forgiveness.

My daughters were out of school for the day, but Patrick wasn't. My routine was off. I was standing in the kitchen, chatting with my daughters, when suddenly I realized I had forgotten to pick up Patrick at the middle school. Panic engulfed me. I was 20 minutes late! That translates to an eternity for an autistic youth who lives by a regimented schedule, who finds comfort and familiarity in his mom circling around in her car and picking him up at the side door of the school each day at exactly 3:20 p.m. (We had worked out that arrangement with the school at the beginning of the year so that Patrick would not have to deal with the sounds and jostling found in the car pickup crowds.)

Lord, please let him be okay. Please let him be settled. Give him peace even though I am horribly late, I prayed.

The school bus lot was deserted. Nobody was milling about the school.

I looked up at the side door, and there was Patrick, staring into the parking lot.

Ugh! What is wrong with me? Why did I forget? I screamed at myself.

Patrick came out and got into the car.

"Patrick, I am so sorry for being late," I said.

"What happened?" he asked.

"Well, the girls were out of school, and I was on a different routine. And I just forgot," I said.

"You *forgot* your son?" he asked.

His question caught me off guard.

That's how it looked to him. He was my son, and I had forgotten him. A mother forgot her son! I wanted to crawl into a hole.

"Patrick, I am sorry," I said. "I didn't mean to forget you. Would you please forgive me?"

I could see his inner struggle. Hurt mixed with compassion for his pitiful mom.

Compassion won out.

"Okay. I will show you mercy," he said.

And he did. I never heard another word about it. It was done. I was forgiven.

I felt like a caged bird that had been set free. I could soar to new heights. I was forgiven!

Patrick was free, too. In fact, he lives a free life—free of bitterness from past hurts and disappointments. He forgives because God tells him to, and he moves on. He presents a beautiful picture of the blessing forgiveness brings into our lives.

Of course, he has had to realize that not everyone eagerly embraces the forgiveness blessing like he does. Once, he did something to upset one of his sisters. When he realized she was upset, he went to her and asked her to forgive him.

Still upset, she huffily answered, "No!"

I heard Patrick protest loudly from the other room, "You can't do that! If someone tells you they are sorry, you have to forgive them! God says so!"

After that episode, we had to have a long talk about how forgiveness is a choice, and everyone makes their own decisions about it.

"Some choices hurt us, and some choices help us," I said.

"Well, I am going to do what God says," Patrick said.

"Good for you!" I said.

When it comes to forgiveness, how I have wished for those I love to "please obey the Lord in what I am saying to you, that it may go well with you and you may live" (Jeremiah 38:20, NASB).

Patrick does that, and he is free!

Patrick's Perspective:

I still choose to forgive people. I have had a lot of moments where it was hard to forgive certain individuals, but I have still decided to forgive, because that is what God says to do. I have been left out, ignored, bullied, abandoned, and criticized. Whenever I go to new places, I am nervous that these things will happen to me again, but I trust God. He helps me to forgive when I need to, and that keeps me free and happy.

SOMETHING TO THINK ABOUT:

Are you finding it difficult to forgive someone?

Would you ask the Lord to help you to forgive?

Would you believe Him that forgiveness sets you free?

17

ENCOUNTERING LOVE THROUGH FAMILY AND FRIENDS

"God places the lonely in families."
—*Psalm 68:6, NIV*

I grew up in a large family. The second-oldest of eight children born within the span of 10 years, I was used to crowds. Growing up, I anesthetized myself against the constant noise and commotion in our home. Once, a power generator strapped to a telephone pole outside our house blew up in the middle of the night after it was hit by lightning. My entire family slept through the boom that was heard across town—loud noises didn't faze us. After my siblings and I married and started having children, family gatherings grew even larger and more clamorous. It wasn't unusual to have almost 50 people arrive to celebrate holidays and special events.

Poor Patrick. The intense noise and activity sent his nervous system into overload. We tried to include him at some of these events, but after several hasty retreats with Patrick kicking and screaming, we decided to let him stay with David's parents, who lived nearby. The majority of our family members lived in northeastern Ohio, so visits had to be well-coordinated to accommodate Patrick's needs. After some trial and error, we soon discovered that Patrick could handle small packs of relatives much better than the entire herd! So, we began to arrange visits with small numbers. Patrick especially enjoyed getting together with his boy cousins and playing video games. I didn't blame him, since he was surrounded by estrogen at home! My heart swelled each time I saw my young nephews bantering and joking with Patrick as they played video games. They would slap him on the back and ask advice on how to get to the higher levels in the games. They started calling Patrick "the Master," since he was so good at the games, a title Patrick relished.

Every summer, Patrick would go to Ohio for about two weeks and stay with my mother, his Grandma Mathie. A loving, gentle soul, she fiercely devoted herself to Patrick while he visited, arranging countless "pack meetings" with his cousins. During his stay, he usually was able to make the rounds to each family's home (10 visits, including my siblings, Mother, Dad and his wife, and David's parents). Patrick learned a great deal about communicating and interacting with others during these visits. I continually thanked the Lord for all my relatives who poured love into Patrick and encouraged their children to do the same.

My mother also had next-door neighbors, the Gooches, who had a son a few years younger than Patrick. This boy, Mookie, and Patrick became fast friends and hung out a lot when Patrick visited. Mookie even got himself out of bed early on the mornings we would head back to North Carolina, so that he could see Patrick off. Patrick has a special place in his heart for all of his Ohio family.

I feel like the Lord went ahead of us in preparing my family's hearts to receive Patrick, and my mother blazed the trail. She worked as communications coordinator and Special Olympics director for the Stark County Board of Mental Retardation in Canton, Ohio. She worked for years to help the handicapped reach their full potential. She says of her work with Special Olympics:

> Once a Special Olympian meets you, they don't forget you, and they are your friend forever. They try their hardest and also cheer on others as they try, no matter what "team" they are on. They overcome some severe physical and emotional issues to better themselves. That keeps coaches and volunteers motivated and inspired as they see the athletes struggle through many obstacles to become the best person they can be. I smiled

going to and from work each day because of the many successes—large and small—that we experienced with our athletes.[ix]

When Patrick came along, my mother was fully prepared for the job of being his grandmother; although, to her, it was not a job, but a labor of love. She and Patrick shared a strong bond. They would walk together, play together, and laugh together. Once, when Mom and Patrick were gliding across a lake in a swan-shaped paddleboat, his grandma quickly urged him, "Patrick! Steer to the right! We are headed for the big fountain in the middle of the lake!" As the spraying water came closer and closer, my mom looked over to see Patrick grinning. "He took me under that water on purpose!" she exclaimed, as she recounted the story to me later, adding, "Do you realize what a good sign that is? That he has a sense of humor like that, being autistic?!" On her birthday that year, Patrick got her a stuffed swan. She keeps the delicate bird perched atop her bed, much to her grandson's delight.

My dad and his wife Kathie have encouraged Patrick, too, taking him to Cleveland Indians' games, and encouraging him in his game design and development activities. His Grandma and Grandpa King have paid him countless visits over the years and encouraged him in his interests as well. Grandpa King sat down with Patrick one swim season and outlined swimming goals for Patrick. Each time Patrick accomplished one of the goals, Grandpa King would send him a reward. Patrick worked hard to reach those milestones. David's brothers Don and Doug also have supported Patrick as "one of the King men," a true brotherhood of affection and loyalty. When our oldest daughter Katie married a handsome, big-hearted young man named Curt Morgan, Patrick instantly had a new "big brother" who hung out with him and encouraged him constantly.

The Lord has given us other family members, not of blood, but of the heart. It became obvious early on that I could no longer take Patrick to church on Wednesday nights. A childcare worker informed me he was too much trouble. That pronouncement, coupled with his continual sensory overloads, prompted me to look for another solution. One Wednesday night, he ran off from me, and when I found him, he was under a table with his eyes pressed tightly shut, his hands over his ears, and his body rocking rhythmically. All the sights, sounds, smells, and jostlings that accompanied Wednesday night suppers and activities were too much for him.

"Let me keep him on Wednesday nights for you," urged Norma, a friendly, kindhearted woman who worked in David's office. Norma lived nearby and loved every one of my children. She even went into the delivery room with me when Sarah was born. She emerged as a special gift from God to an overwhelmed young mother who lived 440 miles away from the nearest relative.

"Are you sure?" I asked.

"Dillon and I would love it," Norma urged. "Besides, you don't want the girls to miss all the fun stuff for the children on Wednesday nights. And you need the break."

That began Patrick's Wednesday nights with the Stacks. Dillon was his buddy, and Norma quickly became his Me-maw. He named her that. Norma and Dillon cherished and accepted Patrick just as he was, and he thrived under their care. When it was time to go to Me-maw and Dillon's house, he eagerly scooped up his favorite toys and headed for the door. Finding someone who can care for your child while you are away is a precious gift, and all good gifts come from God (James 1:17, NASB). I continually thanked the Lord for these heaven-sent members of our family.

If you are the parent of a special needs child, I urge you to accept help from others you trust. The help and support I have received from family and friends have enabled me to be refreshed, restored, and strengthened to continue on this special journey with my son. I know others have been blessed by helping me and my family. "Your children have blessed me more than I ever could have blessed them," Norma told me once when I was thanking her and telling her how much she meant to all of us. If that is true, she must be blessed beyond measure! Then again, that is exactly how God works. He tells us it is more blessed to give than to receive (Acts 20:35, NIV).

I had to have a hysterectomy when my children were 11, 9, 7, and 5. Friends from church stepped in and brought meals for weeks. My girlfriends from China Grove, a group that dubbed itself "The Lunch Bunch," generously brought meals as well and arranged play dates to get my children out of the house for some fun (and much needed rest for Mom).

In 1995, our family welcomed an exchange student Silvana

Milic from Croatia. She attended South Rowan High School and rapidly became a daughter and sister to our family. She and Patrick shared a special bond. When she arrived, Patrick was two years old. She would scoop him up and dance around the living room to "A Whole New World" from Disney's *Aladdin* movie. They share a bond that continues to this day.

All the expressions of love and support I have experienced through family and friends have made me realize how much we need one another. We should never try to go it alone as we face challenges and difficulties. Making and keeping connections with other people help to steer us through the hard times in life. These beautiful souls—whether family or friends—are unexpected blessings that we delightedly discover along the way. We never would have uncovered the depth of their beauty unless we had allowed them to enter our world and become part of it.

Patrick's Perspective:

I love my family so much. They have been so supportive over the years. I know they accept me for who I am, and it is great to be welcomed and loved by them. I still love all my grandparents very much. Even though I do not see Me-maw as much as I used to, she still holds a special place in my heart. It is great to hang out with my cousins, too. They get excited when I come to visit, and that makes me feel good. I am always excited to see them, too. I know God put all these wonderful people in my life. I have felt His love through them. It is amazing!

SOMETHING TO THINK ABOUT:

Who are family and friends for whom you are especially

grateful? Why not write them a note to let them

know how much they are valued?

Would you allow trusted others to help you?

How can they help?

How can you help others?

*Patrick, aka "The Master," playing video games
with cousins Jacob, Isaac, and Jared*

*Croatian exchange student Silvana Milic and Patrick
shared a close bond from the start*

*Silvana with the King children Emily,
Katie, Sarah, and Patrick
(Photo by Karen Goforth)*

Norma ("Me-maw") and Patrick

Dillon and Patrick

Patrick having fun with his Ohio friend Mookie

Patrick and Grandma Mathie in the infamous swan

*Grandma Mathie displaying the stuffed swan
given to her by Patrick*

*Curt Morgan (center) became a great brother-in-law and
mentor to Patrick when he married Patrick's sister Katie
(Photo by Sassyfras Studios)*

Patrick, Sarah, and Emily with Grandma and Grandpa King

Patrick at his graduation with Grandpa Mathie
and his wife Kathie

18

NOTICING THE DETAILS

"For since the creation of the world His invisible attributes,
His eternal power and divine nature, have been clearly seen,
being understood through what has been made."
—Romans 1:20, NASB

When David and I decided to take a much-needed vacation out of town, we enlisted our dear friend Norma to stay with our children at our house. We gave everyone strict instructions about the rules while we were gone, and at the top of the list for the girls was, "No boyfriends!" We didn't want Norma to have to be concerned about supervising the activities of hormone-driven teenagers while we were out of town. Let's face it, love is a powerful force that can lead us to do crazy things. Which is exactly what happened.

One evening, Patrick walked down the stairs to the basement, where the television and his bedroom were located. He found one of his sisters sitting on the couch watching the TV.

He stopped abruptly and said to her, "Where is he?"

"Where is who?" she asked innocently.

"Your boyfriend. I know he's here," Patrick said.

"How could you know that?" she asked, pretending to be confused.

Patrick looked directly at her and pronounced, "I can smell him."

He had her there. Everyone in the family knew about Patrick's keen sense of smell. From a young age, he would pull the front of his shirt up over his nose if a particular scent displeased him. He would warn us of olfactory invasions long before they registered an impression in our nostrils. When one of our friends gave him a ride to school, he informed her that her car "smelled like a baby" as he held his shirt over his nose. She pulled her car over to the side of the road and promptly put her lunch bag in the trunk. Patrick's nose had registered the unpleasant odor of her hard-boiled eggs!

"I really can smell him," Patrick said again to his sister.

The door creaked as my daughter's boyfriend sheepishly emerged from the game closet.

"Please don't tell Mom and Dad! I'll give you a dollar if you don't tell," my daughter begged.

"Okay," said Patrick, sealing the deal.

As David and I returned from our trip, we had no more than laid our luggage on the kitchen floor when Patrick came running into the room, informing us that our daughter had snuck her boyfriend over while we were gone.

"Patrick!" she exclaimed. "You promised you wouldn't tell!"

"But you never gave me the dollar," he said.

In Patrick's rules-oriented world, he got to tell because the deal was contingent on both parties keeping their part of the bargain. He wasn't being mean, just literal.

We laughed about that story for years. We still do. Everyone except the daughter who was caught in her offense. She had to suffer the consequences of disobeying her parents. For the rest of us, it reinforced Patrick's sense of justice, and his unique gifts in the sensory department. You keep your word when you give it. You follow the rules. And you notice everything in creation through the strong senses God gave you.

All creation speaks of the glory of God (Job 12:7-10, Psalm 19:1-2, NASB). Our senses pull us into noticing and appreciating everything God has made, and hopefully the God who made everything. With his heightened senses, Patrick constantly registered and shared God's creative presence in the world. We would be walking outside, and Patrick would draw us aside to notice a delicate purple violet stretching toward the sun out of the crack in a sidewalk. He would lead us by the hand to inhale the delicate perfumes of flowers. He would point out the beautiful melodies in the background music in a waiting room. He would warn us when a mosquito was within a 500-yard range of us! He continually reminded us of the many intricacies of God's beautiful creation. The Lord meant for us to enjoy these things and to show us His glory in them. He is an awesome Creator, and Patrick helps to remind us of that.

Too many times, I find myself getting caught up in the activities of every day, speeding through my "to do" list without pausing to notice the delightful evidences of the Lord all around me. Patrick teaches me to slow down and smell the roses in life. It is a lesson that would benefit all of us.

Patrick's Perspective:

Even though I have had problems with my senses in the past, I find them beneficial at times. Sometimes it is annoying if I am having a conversation with someone, and my ears pick up a conversation on the other side of the room. I always hear a lot of background noise, which is one of the things that makes it hard for me to talk with others. It is like if you were trying to talk with someone and your TV is on the highest volume, the radio is playing, and your computer is running a video.

But there are also blessings to my extra sensitive hearing. I can hear all the many details in music when I'm learning to sing it. It is easy for me to learn music quickly because of my keen sense of hearing. I only have to listen to it a couple times, and I know it and can repeat it. One of the music professors at Pfeiffer University played music on a piano, and he wanted me to repeat those notes. It kept getting harder and harder, but I could do it. I am grateful to experience the world, especially music, through my senses. I like to go outside and spend time in nature. It relaxes me, and I like to notice all the incredible things God has made.

SOMETHING TO THINK ABOUT:

Do you regularly take time to slow down and

appreciate the beauty in the world around you?

Consider taking some time to go outside and smell some of the flowers

you encounter, to close your eyes and listen to the sounds of nature, to feel

the breeze against your face or the warm sun on your cheek.

Pick up a flower, leaf, or blade of grass. Study its intricate details,

and feel the sensation of it between your fingers.

Play some music, and keenly listen to each note. Thank God for

allowing you to experience through your senses all He has made.

SUSAN JANE KING

19

DETERMINING TO KEEP
GOING WITH GOD

"Let us run with endurance the race that is set before us."
—Hebrews 12:1, NASB

Patrick joined the South Rowan High School swim team as a freshman. He was extremely uncoordinated and about 60 pounds overweight. But he wanted to swim like his sisters Emily and Sarah. He wanted to be part of a team.

"Maybe he can be sort of a 'mascot' for the team," David said.

I was proud of Patrick for wanting to try, but I had my reservations. I had been to plenty of swim meets with my daughters. The strong smell of chlorine permeated the pool area and assaulted your nostrils. High humidity often made spectators wringing wet with sweat. The combination of chlorine and heat gave me a continuous headache, until I learned to pop two ibuprofen before every meet.

I thought about Patrick's physical limitations. Could he even learn the strokes and swim techniques? Could he survive the endless drills that strained mind and body?

I remembered when I took him for swim lessons at the local Y. I had called ahead and had explained Patrick's unique needs to the aquatics director, who had graciously received him into their program. He also selected a swimming instructor for Patrick who happened to be a special needs teacher in the local school system.

"There are new studies out that show a correlation between

the hand over hand movement of the swimming strokes and improved brain activity in autistic individuals," she told me. "Keep your son in swimming."

"Okay. Let's give it a try," I said to Patrick.

Greg Yanz, the Raiders' swim coach, welcomed Patrick into the world of aquatics. He challenged Patrick to improve and worked with him long after the other swimmers left the pool deck. He gave my son a chance.

"I can't dive off the block," Patrick said in frustration, after the first several practices. "I can't get my legs to do what my brain is telling them to do."

But he didn't give up.

"God is telling me to keep trying," Patrick said. Taking that directive to heart, he stayed after practice for two years straight, trying to get his legs in line with his brain.

We attended his swim meets, watching him stand on the edge of the pool, instead of the block, at the beginning of each race and belly flop into the water, rising from the water one or two body lengths behind the other 5 to 7 swimmers in each heat.

At the end of each race, he would check with the timekeepers to see if he had cut any time off of his race. The shaving of one or two seconds resulted in extreme exuberance.

I loved his heart.

At the beginning of his sophomore year, he came up to me after school one day and said, "Mom, I'm fat, and I need to lose weight."

I looked at him, shocked.

"What? Why do you say that?" I asked, caught off guard.

"We watched a videotape of our chorus concert in class today, and I could see it. I am definitely fat," he said.

"Wow!" I thought. When my daughters would make similar pronouncements, the words were always accompanied by tears and derogatory comments about how "ugly" they looked. Here was Patrick making a simple presentation of the facts and his desire to do something about them.

"So, I want you to teach me about the Weight Watchers program," he continued.

"I think it would help me lose weight, and if I lose weight, I think I could do better at swimming, too. And I want to get a lot better at swimming."

"Okay," I said.

I was quite familiar with the Weight Watchers program. I had followed it for years. The booklets, slide rules, and calculators associated with the program occupied drawers and shelves throughout our home. The Dining Out companion book traveled with us everywhere in the glove compartment of my van. When our daughters had wanted to lose weight, I focused them on a healthy lifestyle, teaching them the Weight Watchers principles. My Iron Man athletic husband never had to follow Weight Watchers, but the rest of us pledged allegiance to the Weight Watchers principles. Now Patrick was joining the fold. I taught him all the rules of the program, and he followed them as if his life depended on it.

I admired his self-discipline. He didn't waver. Once, we were having a birthday celebration, and he politely declined eating the cake (one of his favorites) because he had already used up his points allowance for that day. He embraced the ideas of drinking eight glasses of water a day and making sure he ate enough fruits and vegetables. His literalness and need for a routine blended well with the Weight Watchers structure. His adherence to the program was even comical at times.

"Mom," he said one evening. "I have good news and bad news."

"What is it?" I asked.

"The good news is that I made an A on my math test today," he announced.

"That's great! I am so proud of you," I said. "What's the bad news?"

"The bad news is I'm as hungry as a beast, and I'm all out of points!" Patrick said.

Through his foray into Weight Watchers, he lost 60 pounds! He hardly looked like the same young man who entered the pool at around 200 pounds. When he climbed atop the block at the Pfeiffer University Invitational Swim Meet toward the end of his sophomore year, I held my breath. What was he doing on the block!? He usually jumped off the side of the pool. To my amazement, when the starting buzzer rang, my slim, athletic son raised his arms in the air, linked his hands together, bent over, and dove into the pool! David and I and the South Rowan parents erupted into loud cheers and applause. In our opinion, the race was already won.

Patrick swam the 200- and 500-yard freestyle events for his team. They are called the endurance races, and that's what he did. He endured. He didn't give up. He swam over the summer between his sophomore and junior years. He was determined to get better, faster in the water. Every day, I would take him to the pool to swim laps, and he would call me two hours later to come pick him up. When swim season started that year, I noticed he looked stronger, more agile in the water. He glided through the water with power and precision. The seconds were dropping off his times in a rapid progression.

He had his own routine at the pool. He took a folding sports chair from our home and set it up away from the crowds and his team on the pool deck. He would go to his chair when sounds and sensations became too much for him. I always bought him a heat sheet, which listed all the races and the swimmers who were competing in each event. He followed the heat sheet like a road map in order to navigate through everything that was happening around him. He made sure he was in place to start his races on time, even if it meant going up to the starting block area and waiting through two or more races until it was his turn.

"I love coaching your son," Coach Yanz said. "He just might be the most coachable student I have ever had in my 16 years of coaching swimming and baseball. Whatever you ask him to do, he does it, without complaining, without questions. And he works to make the swim intervals I give him, or he's going to die trying. I am so glad to have him on the team. He is a great role model for the other swimmers."

Patrick. A role model!

Lord, You are full of surprises! I thought with delight.

When the conference swim meet arrived, I joined the mob of other South Rowan parents sporting our black and red apparel in the bleachers at the J.F. Hurley Y in Salisbury. I scanned the pool lanes where the swimmers were warming up and found the familiar form of my son, arcing through the water.

Lord, help him to have a good day. Help him to sense Your presence with him. And help him to honor You in everything he does here, I silently prayed.

After Patrick climbed out of the water and made his way to his chair, I walked over to check on him.

"How's it going, Patrick?" I asked.

"Good. Can you pray with me?" he inquired.

Prayer was at the core of everything Patrick did.

If he had a test, he prayed. If he had to write a paper, he prayed. If he had a concert coming up for his chorus class, he prayed. If he had trouble understanding people, he prayed. If he felt lonely, he prayed. And especially, if he had a swim meet, he prayed. This was the big one.

"I just don't want to let down my coaches or team," he said.

So we prayed.

Patrick always brought the palms of his hands together, fingers facing upward, positioned directly in front of his bowed head when he prayed. He did that now.

I put my hand on his shoulder and said, *"Lord, here we are at the conference swim meet. It's a big meet for Patrick and his team. We thank You that You are here with Patrick and with each one of the swimmers on his team. We ask You to help Patrick today to swim his very best. We ask You to help him feel Your presence with him as he swims. We ask You to give him the strength he needs to do his best. We ask for Your peace and for joy in swimming here today. Lord, we ask You to bless him, but most of all, we ask that he might be a blessing to others here today, his teammates, his coaches, parents, and others who are here at the pool. Let him swim for Your glory. In Jesus' name. Amen."*

"Thank you, Mom," Patrick said.

"I am so proud of you," I said.

He flashed me his characteristic sweet smile.

"Well, I guess I had better go," he said.

"Go get 'em," I urged, giving him a thumbs-up.

He flashed me a thumbs-up of his own and started toward the blocks.

"How's Patrick doing today?" asked my friend Cindy, whose daughter Kristina not only swam with Patrick but also belonged to a circle of Patrick's closest friends on the team.

"He seems good today," I said. "Thanks for asking."

Cindy, like other parents, had witnessed Patrick's trials, tribulations, and triumphs in the pool. She knew it only took a slight deviation from the way Patrick thought things ought to go to send him spinning off into anxiety and uncertainty.

"I've been praying for him," Cindy said.

I thanked God for this dear friend. I knew prayers like hers had been answered over the years, and I treasured every one of them.

"Thank you. That means so much to me," I said. "How's Kristina doing?"

"She's a little tired. They had to get here kind of early," Cindy said. "But she's excited, too."

Kindhearted and sweet, Kristina lived down the lane almost directly across the street from our house. She had given Patrick rides to and from school and swim practice for countless months, as driving was still too intimidating for him.

The swim team had rapidly emerged as a second family to Patrick. I looked over at Caleb, another member of Patrick's inner circle, pumping up and encouraging the other juniors on the team. I gazed at Jeremiah, Patrick's friendly rival. They shared a mutual admiration for one another as they battled to pass each other in the endurance events at each meet. There was Reynold, whom David and Patrick had dubbed "the torpedo." And there was McKinney, appearing shy, but boasting pictures of mudding with four-wheelers on her Facebook page.

An inspiring leader, Caleb had started inviting this particular group over to his house toward the middle of the year. Patrick was thrilled to be invited. I thanked the Lord repeatedly for giving Caleb a heart for Patrick, and for being a great role model for him. The "sensational six," as I called them, watched movies, played "Capture the Flag," and had bonfires together. Patrick's prayers often included this special group of friends.

He had come a long way from the days of withdrawing and avoiding people. Now, he wanted to have friends and be part of things. I prayed each one of them would have a blessed day at the meet.

Patrick stood on the block directly beside Jeremiah, ready to enter the pool for the 200 freestyle swim. He intently focused on the lane in front of him.

Light flashed and the buzzer pierced the air to signal the start of the race. The swimmers dove into the water like a bolt of lightning. Patrick came up from his dive and leveled out on the surface of the water, his arms forming the familiar arcs and dips associated with stroking, while his feet churned the water with continual kicks. He approached the wall to make his first flip turn and flipped—too early. I caught my breath. Something was off. I strained to get a closer look at Patrick, and then I saw it. His goggles were tangled around his neck, flopping aimlessly in the water.

"His goggles came off!" I told Cindy, alarmed.

"Oh no!" she said.

We both knew dislodged goggles were a challenge for any swimmer. You can't see the wall clearly to make your turns. Good turns are critical to good times. Patrick had worked relentlessly on his turns, attempting to spring off the wall like a rapidly dislodged bullet out of a gun barrel.

My heart sank. Patrick had worked so hard to get to this race, and I could tell he was struggling. I watched him misjudge the location of the wall on several more turns. I saw him slip behind the race leaders.

Lord, please help him. Give him strength. Guide him through this challenge, I prayed.

Patrick finished third, behind a young man from East Rowan and his teammate Jeremiah.

As he pulled himself from the pool, his shoulders and head were drooping. He reached up and yanked the goggles from around his neck and pummeled them onto the pool deck.

I found him in his chair with his head in his hands.

"Patrick," I said gently.

He raised his head with an anguished look.

"I let down my team, Mom. I let down my team," he said, his voice shaking.

"No you didn't. You got third place. The team gets points for third place, Patrick," I reassured him.

"No. Our coach said only first and second places get points," Patrick said. "I HATE that my goggles came off. I'm really mad about that!"

"I don't blame you for being mad. I would be mad, too," I said. "But I am super proud of you for doing your best when you had that challenge. I think you did great!"

I patted his back and felt his shoulders relax under my hand.

I knew he never wanted to disappoint his parents, either.

"Listen," I added. "I think we should go talk to your Assistant Coach Gosha over there and ask him about the points. I really think you did earn some points for your team with third place."

"Okay," Patrick relented.

We found Joe Gosha at the team's scoring table. I explained to him Patrick's concerns and his feelings about letting down the team.

"Patrick, you definitely earned some great points for us," Gosha said. "You did exactly what we wanted you to do. What Coach Yanz was talking about when he mentioned first and second place finishes is that those swimmers get named to the All-Conference Swim Team. You definitely did a great job out there for us!"

Patrick visibly relaxed.

"Now, what we need you to do is to focus on your 500 freestyle race," Gosha said. "And Patrick, you could win that race. You have it in you. Go out there, and give it your best."

I saw Patrick take in those words like marching orders.

"Okay! I will swim hard, Coach," he said. "I will do my best!"

"You always do, Patrick. And that's what I admire about you," Gosha said.

I was silently praising God for this wonderful man who was painting a picture of strength and accomplishment for my son.

"Mom," said Patrick when we got back to his chair, "we forgot to pray that my goggles wouldn't come off."

I grinned. "You're right, Son. We'll pray that before the next race."

Prior to the start of the 500 freestyle, Patrick motioned me to come talk with him.

"Mom, I'm so tired," he said. "I don't know why. I just feel so tired. Maybe it's because I got upset. I just want to do really well in the 500 race. Could we pray again?"

"Of course," I said.

"Lord, You know Patrick is really tired right now. But You promise that when we're weak, that's when Your strength is made perfect. That's when You show up and reveal how strong YOU are. Do that now for Patrick. Give him Your supernatural strength to swim this next race. Let him feel Your strength moving through him with every kick, every stroke, every turn. Let everyone here see how strong You are and how Your power is perfected in weakness. And allow Patrick to feel so strong that he has joy swimming this race, swimming with You. And, Lord, please help his goggles to stay on!"

Patrick grinned at the close of my prayer.

"Thanks, Mom," he said.

"It's going to be awesome!" I said. "I can't wait to see what God does!"

Patrick kept grinning.

I rejoined Cindy in the bleachers.

"Is Patrick okay?" she asked.

"He's just really tired," I said. "Please pray for him."

"I certainly will," Cindy said.

At the start of the 500-yard freestyle, Patrick stood on the block alongside Jeremiah again, with his same laser gaze on the lane in front of him.

After the light flash and buzzer, he leaped off the block to begin the first of 10 long laps in the pool. He and Jeremiah paced one another, trading strokes and positions for the first half of the race.

Then, something happened. To my amazement, I watched Patrick start to move away from Jeremiah, extending the distance between them, moving farther and farther ahead in the pool. His arms moved rhythmically through the water. His feet kicked furiously. His flip turns propelled him through the water like a missile. He was pulling way ahead. He was *winning* the race!

I stood up and started screaming, cheering loudly for Patrick.

David would always tease me, "He can't hear you with all that splashing going on."

"I know!" I would tell him. "It isn't for him. It's for me!"

Cheering gave voice to the pressure, the intensity of the moment. It gave wings to my elation.

"Go Patrick! Go Patrick! Go!"

He was sailing through the water, steering his ship to victory, like a sailboat speeding through an armada race.

He was a pool length ahead of all the other swimmers.

Cindy and I looked at each other in amazement.

"He's going to win! He's going to win!" she shouted.

Patrick extended his arm and plunged into the touch pad at the end of the race.

The scoreboard clicked the number "1" in the place position beside his lane.

Patrick looked up to check his time and position on the scoreboard.

Shock and elation broke out across his face.

His teammates and coaches were cheering and raising their fists in the air. The parents around me were screaming wildly.

Tears flowed down my cheeks as I realized what had just happened.

Patrick had just WON the Conference Swim Meet in the 500 freestyle.

I watched as his teammates engulfed him when he rounded the corner away from the blocks. I saw his coaches slap him on the back and shake his hand. I observed the officials slide the gold medal over his head. And I praised God for the miracle I had just witnessed.

"Mom," he told me when I reached him to congratulate him. "Right in the middle of the race, I felt this incredible strength fill my whole body. It was just like we prayed. God did it!"

"Yes, He did!" I told Patrick. "And I am proud of you for letting Him do it through you.

"We should pray and thank God for what He did," I added.

"I already did," Patrick said, "But we can thank Him again, because you never can thank God enough."

We stood in the middle of the pool deck as Patrick bowed his head and brought his hands up to pray. I knew a lot of people were watching us, and I was glad.

After we raised our heads, I pulled out my cellphone and snapped a picture of Patrick with his medal to send to David, who was working that day. "Guess who just WON the Conference in the 500 freestyle!" I texted.

I felt a tap on my shoulder.

I looked around to see an elderly gentleman sporting an enormous camera.

I recognized him immediately. He owned a photo studio in town and took pictures of the team every season. We had shared a long conversation after Patrick's freshman picture session.

"He was scared to death about the picture session. It was as if he didn't know what to do," he had told me.

I had then confided in him about Patrick's autism and the challenge of unfamiliar situations.

I remembered Patrick's freshman swim photo, with his strained smile and his foot awkwardly placed on the step to the block.

"Is that your son? The boy who just won the 500?" he asked me.

"Yes, that's him," I answered.

"He has autism, right?" he asked softly.

"Yes," I said.

His eyes filled with tears, and he motioned for me to come closer.

"My 3-year-old grandson was just diagnosed with autism," he whispered, overcome with emotion. "It, it . . . "

"It gives you hope, doesn't it?" I asked gently.

Unable to speak, he simply nodded his head.

"Nothing is impossible with God," I told him, smiling and placing my hand on his shoulder.

"Thank you," he said.

As he walked away, I prayed, *Lord, please encourage that dear man and his family. Comfort them, and give them strength. And, Lord, please allow Patrick and me to encourage other people like this man who are dealing with autism. Use us to let other people know that there is always hope with You.*

Patrick's swimming continued to improve. By his senior year, he won nearly every race he swam, whether in the 200- or 500-yard freestyles. He also began swimming in some relay races for the team. By the time he finished his senior swim season, he had won both the 200 and 500 freestyle races at the county and conference competitions and had qualified to the regional swim meet in the 500.

"Let us run with endurance the race that is set before us, fixing our eyes on Jesus, the author and perfecter of faith" (Hebrews 12:1-2, NASB). In the pool and in life, Patrick would not give up. He kept looking to Jesus to help him in every way. Despite his many challenges, he just kept on with Jesus, and the result was miraculous!

We were just climbing into bed after the conclusion of the Regional Swim Meet when our phone rang. It was Coach Yanz.

I handed the phone to David.

"Really!" David said. "What did he say? What should we do? Okay. Thanks for calling and telling us."

"What was that all about?" I asked.

"Coach Yanz said the swim coach at Pfeiffer University came up to him after the meet and said, 'Tell me about this King kid. I'm interested in him for our swim team,'" David said.

"What!" I exclaimed.

A college is interested in Patrick swimming for them! I couldn't wrap my mind around the idea of Patrick swimming in college. I had never even imagined the possibility.

A Division II school, Pfeiffer University was nestled in the quaint village of Misenheimer, about a 30-minute drive from our home. We passed through it every time we drove down Highway 52 on our way to the beach.

"Coach Yanz said we should call the coach at Pfeiffer if we are interested in talking with him. His name is Eric Anderson. We can find him on the school Web site," David continued. "Susan, this is big. It's a great opportunity. I think we should look into it. And I have to tell you, I just haven't been comfortable with the idea of Patrick going to UNC-Charlotte. I think it's way too big and intimidating for him. I think he'll get overwhelmed in the sheer mass of students there. I have been praying about it, and I think this is an answer to those prayers."

The University of North Carolina at Charlotte featured a huge, sprawling campus situated on the edge of North Carolina's largest city. Classrooms filled with hundreds of students were commonplace. Patrick had chosen UNCC because it offered an impressive major in video game design, which he wanted to pursue.

But after his acceptance and the days got closer for him to attend college, an uneasiness had settled upon David and me. Maybe the apprehension had something to do with the Lord pointing us in another direction.

I contacted Coach Anderson and arranged for Patrick, David, and me to visit Pfeiffer. As we drove into the campus, I was charmed by the warm and welcoming feeling exuded by the colonial brick buildings and neatly manicured lawns. The chapel spire stood white and dominant against an azure sky.

As we approached the entrance to Merner Gymnasium, where the pool was located and where Coach Anderson had his office, we noticed a yellow flyer attached to the door. It had the school's mascot, the falcon, in the left corner, and it read, "Patrick King. Hometown: China Grove, NC. Goal: To Become The Next Falcon Swimmer. Welcome to Pfeiffer!"

"Oh my gosh! They have my name on the door!" Patrick chuckled, the corners of his mouth turning up in a smile.

"That's awesome, Bub!" said David, using our special term of endearment for Patrick.

We swung through the doors and headed to the coach's office.

"Patrick!" Coach Anderson said in a hearty welcome.

He came out from behind his desk and grasped Patrick's hand firmly in a handshake. A tall, muscular man with bright, dancing eyes, Coach Anderson exuded strength and cheerfulness as he welcomed us. He greeted me and David with the same openness and settled the three of us on the couch for a chat.

"This is Katie Huff," Coach Anderson said as we were introduced to an athletic-looking blonde with a charming smile.

"Katie actually was the first one to notice Patrick, when we had our invitational swim meet here in the winter. Patrick asked her to hold his glasses while he swam, and she was enchanted by that. Then, when she saw him swim, she said we ought to consider him for our swim team. We have been watching his performances since then."

Katie smiled as Coach Anderson retold the story. So did Patrick.

"I want to tell you that we want you to swim at Pfeiffer. We want you on our swim team, Patrick, and we would like to offer you a scholarship to swim here," Coach Anderson said.

Patrick's eyes got as big as saucers.

"What do you think about that?" Coach Anderson asked.

"Well," Patrick paused. "It's going to be hard."

"You're right," Coach Anderson replied. "And I am glad you know that up front. It is important to be realistic about what's involved with swimming on a college team. It is a lot of work, but it can be very rewarding, too."

I could see Patrick hesitating, trying to find the words he wanted to speak.

"He is afraid of disappointing you," I said.

From all my years of watching him swim, I knew that disappointing his coaches was his greatest fear. He wanted to do well for them.

I saw Patrick look at the coach tentatively after I said those words.

"There's something you need to know, Patrick," Coach Anderson said. "You will never disappoint me as long as I know you are doing your best. And from what I've heard from your high school coach, you always give your best. I think your positive attitude and strong work ethic would be a real asset to our team."

He went on to talk about how the swim team was a "family" at Pfeiffer, that they did things together socially, often lived in the same dorm, and supported one another on and off the pool deck. I realized the swim team could play a major role in helping Patrick transition to college.

We then met with an admissions counselor, who discussed academic majors at Pfeiffer. She said Patrick qualified for a Presidential Academic Scholarship, based on his grades in high school. She also encouraged Patrick to apply to the university and if he was accepted, to attend Accepted Students Day, where he could interview for additional scholarships. Lastly, we took a campus tour and ate in the cafeteria.

"What do you think, Patrick?" David asked as we were driving back home.

"I really like it," Patrick said. "I think I should go there."

David and I looked at one another and smiled.

"What about swimming?" I asked.

"I think I should join the swim team," Patrick said. Remembering Coach Anderson's comments, he added, "And I am going to work hard and do my best."

He emailed Coach Anderson with the news when we got home.

"That is the best news I've heard today! You just made my week!" Coach Anderson replied. "I will get you some swim team information soon. Welcome to Pfeiffer!"

I was so grateful the Lord had redirected our steps and had led us to Pfeiffer University. It seemed like the perfect atmosphere for Patrick. Small. Manageable. Supportive. And there already were people on campus who not only appreciated him but actually *liked* him. Patrick had a way about him, a sincere, caring nature that respected others, and he gave honest, heartfelt words when the need arose. He never wanted to hurt anyone, and he loved to encourage others when he could. I saw those traits endearing him to many along life's road.

Patrick kept swimming the summer after his senior year in high school, trying to stay in shape for college swimming. When college started, he rapidly entered the world of college athletics, swimming twice a day on weekdays and once on Saturday mornings. On many days, he spent three hours in the pool and gym, in addition to attending classes and doing homework.

Some days when I would call him, he would wearily announce, "I'm so tired!" On other days, he would excitedly say, "I met all my intervals in practice today!"

Patrick struggled through the swim season, frequently discouraged because his swim times were not what he wanted them to be. He dropped almost 20 pounds his first semester because he was burning so many calories in the pool and he could not find a lot of food he liked in the cafeteria. Someone told him he needed to be consuming more protein, so he was eating hamburger patties for every meal! He finally related his food issues to us in January, and we helped him seek assistance. The dean of students and director of food services personally met with him to facilitate solutions to his dietary issues. They helped Patrick develop a list of foods he liked. They encouraged Patrick to see the director of food services in the cafeteria each morning and let him know what Patrick wanted to eat that day, and the cafeteria staff would prepare those foods for him.

At Pfeiffer, Patrick continued to swim the endurance events, which included the 500-yard, the 1000-yard, and the mile freestyles. He attended every practice and meet and just kept swimming. By the time he went to the Bluegrass Conference Collegiate Swim Meet in Charlotte, North Carolina, in February 2013, his times still had not dropped like he wanted. I climbed into the stands to watch him swim his 1000 freestyle, awestruck by the caliber of swimmers walking around the pool deck. Each swimmer looked like a finely tuned swimming machine, with taut muscles and sculpted bodies.

Patrick, too, had grown leaner and stronger. I could tell. What I enjoyed most was watching him interact with his teammates, joking, talking, and smiling. He belonged on the team. My heart swelled with joy. As he climbed atop the starting block, my mind drifted back to other conference swim meets. He had come a long way since then. His swimming times were about the same, but he had matured, gaining confidence and the inner strength that comes from choosing to trust God over and over.

The starting horn sounded, and I watched Patrick slice into the water and begin his strokes. He glided through the water effortlessly, and much faster than I remembered. As I watched his times flash on the screen at the end of each lap, I realized he was cutting major time off of his swim. His friend George looked up at me and gave me a thumbs-up. "He's going to have his best swim ever!" he said. When Patrick finally plunged his hand into the touch pad at the end of the race, he had cut 47 seconds off of his best time for the year. His teammates buzzed around him like a swarm of bees, excitedly patting him on the back and cheering his success. Coach Anderson came up and high-fived him, as Patrick grinned from ear to ear. And he didn't stop there. He cut 26 seconds off his 500 and 10 seconds off his 200 swim later that weekend. Patrick got to experience the progress he had longed for all year.

As I reflected on the weekend's events, I thanked God for giving Patrick the opportunity to swim in college. What a surprise! *I never could have imagined anything like this, Lord!* I prayed. *Thank You for allowing Patrick to swim, to make friends, and to experience results from his hard work. Your grace is amazing!*

Other people were noticing his accomplishments, too. At the end-of-year banquet for the swim team, Coach Anderson gave Patrick the "You Motivate Me" Award. And, at the end-of-year Athletic Awards Ceremony for all athletic teams at Pfeiffer University, Patrick received the "Perseverance Award," which was voted on by his peers from all the athletic teams.

I asked Eric Anderson, Head Swimming Coach at Pfeiffer University, if he would like to make some comments about Patrick for this book. Here is what he said:

> Patrick King has given me perspective. Every day that I have the opportunity to work with Patrick, he reminds me of all that is good in the world. I see Patrick take everything he faces head-on with everything he has. Over the last year, I have gotten to know Patrick through working with him on the swim team at Pfeiffer University. We 'accidentally' found Patrick at one of our high school invitational swim meets. We knew he wouldn't be the fastest kid on the team, but also knew that he would bring something to the table. We were right! Patrick helps the team by getting very high marks in all of his classes, leads by example in the pool by always giving his best on

every set he swims, and most of all, Patrick spreads his enthusiasm for life with his teammates. I know that my experience with having Patrick on the team has far exceeded what I thought I would experience with him. If I come to the pool after a hard day in the office, I can look at Patrick, say something, and he always gives me the double thumbs-up. He keeps me on an even keel and reminds me that I need to focus on the good in every situation that presents itself. As for Patrick's experiences...I would say that Patrick grew up quite a bit this past year in his first season of collegiate swimming. I believe that Patrick gained as much direction and support from his teammates as he gave them. Our team was easily better having Patrick King as a member. I look forward to having him as an alumnus of my program someday.[x]

Patrick's Perspective:

Swimming definitely has changed my life. I cannot imagine where I would be if I did not swim. Swimming is what got me to Pfeiffer. Swimming is what taught me to persevere. I have made some amazing friends through swimming, and I have experienced joy in my accomplishments. My coaches have encouraged me and have been great role models for me. At times, I thought about quitting swimming in college because it was so hard, but I felt God telling me to keep going and it would get better.

God taught me that "I can do all things through Christ who strengthens me" (Philippians 4:13, NASB). I have learned that if God wants you to do something, He will give you the power to do it. I felt like God wanted me to join the swim team when I went to high school, so I did it. At first, it was challenging, and I had a hard time getting my body to do the things I wanted it to.

I kept working at my swimming. That was my routine. My autism helped me with this. I swim the endurance events, which involve swimming laps over and over. This trait enabled me to win the county and conference 200 and 500 freestyle events, to qualify to Regionals, and to get recruited to swim at

Pfeiffer University, even receiving a scholarship to swim there! Only God could take an overweight, uncoordinated autistic boy and turn him into a championship swimmer who got a college scholarship!

I do not think we should ever give up if God asks us to do something, because He is the One who does it anyway! He can do anything He wants to because He's God!

SOMETHING TO THINK ABOUT:

Where might the Lord be telling you to keep going?

Will you rely on Him to give you the strength to do so?

Will you believe that God has blessings

for you if you persevere?

*Patrick ready to dive off the block, after
working for 2 years to master the task*

*Patrick celebrating after
improving his swim times*

Patrick's characteristic smile after winning an event

Patrick bringing home the gold

Patrick and Jeremiah

Patrick and Caleb

Patrick and Coach Yanz

*Patrick with Coach Anderson during Patrick's
recruitment visit to Pfeiffer University*

*Patrick flanked by his parents at his official signing with
Pfeiffer University. Back row: South Rowan Assistant Swim
Coach Jacob Morton, and Head Swim Coach Greg Yanz.*

Patrick on the swim deck at the Pfeiffer University pool

Patrick swimming practice laps at Pfeiffer

20

BEING WELCOMED TO THE TABLE

"He hath made us accepted in the beloved."
—Ephesians 1:6, KJV

"**M**om, I don't want to go to school today," Patrick said, shuffling his feet back and forth, looking at the ground.

"Why not?" I asked.

It was Patrick's second week of high school, a big change for him, and for us.

He looked up at me with sadness and dejection.

"I'm so lonely, Mom. Nobody talks to me. They all look at me like I'm weird. And I don't have anyone to sit with in the cafeteria. I just sit out in the hallway on a bench and eat my lunch."

Sorrow swept over me as I pictured him in the hallway on a bench by himself, slowly eating food off his cafeteria tray. Finding a place at the lunch table had been a challenge for all four of my children, but especially Patrick, who struggled socially. He agonized over how to talk with people and how to read their complicated facial expressions and body language. Signals easily understood by most of us become confusing indicators to those with autism.

"I want to make friends, but I don't know how to do it," he agonized.

"Let's pray about it," I urged, placing my hand on his shoulder. *"Dear Lord, Patrick is lonely. Please help him. Give him a place to sit at lunch with friends who welcome him to their table. Bring good friends into his life, and help him to be a good friend, too. You know exactly what Patrick needs, and we are counting on You to provide it. Thank You that You made him special and unique, that You smile when You look at him. Help him to realize how much You love him. Let him experience Your love through other people, and empower him to love others in Your name. Amen."*

Patrick headed off to school, and I reached for the phone.

"May I speak with Jan Gore, please?" I asked the receptionist at South Rowan High School.

"Jan Gore . . . ," I heard his chorus teacher announce at the other end of the phone line.

I had felt the Lord impress on me to call her once Patrick had left. I explained the situation, knowing that Patrick's lunch period fell halfway through his chorus class.

"Do you think you could ask some chorus students to invite Patrick to sit with them during lunch?" I asked. "And it would be fine if you want to explain to them a little about Patrick's autism. It might help them understand him better."

"I had no idea this was happening!" Mrs. Gore said. "I will definitely take care of it. I'll send Patrick to the guidance office for something, explain everything to the class, and ask some students to volunteer to include him at lunch. We are a family here in the chorus, and we take care of our own."

I knew Mrs. Gore had stayed true to her word when Patrick walked in the door from school that day. He was smiling and animated as he laid his book bag on the kitchen table.

"How was school today?" I asked.

"Awesome!" he said with a big smile.

"A couple kids from chorus invited me to sit with them at their lunch table, and they even talked to me!" he said.

Thank you, Lord, I prayed.

Over the next few months, I watched Patrick become increasingly involved with his chorus friends. He continued to sit with them at lunch and talked about them at home. Eventually, he invited them to come over to the house, and they accepted, spending countless hours laughing, talking, playing video games, and watching movies. They would pile into cars after chorus concerts and head out to a local restaurant to eat, hang out, and celebrate their accomplishments. He had a similar group of friends on the swim team, too. My heart radiated with joy every time I saw Patrick having fun with others.

All of us want to be accepted, valued, and included. The Lord wired that into us so that we could learn that we are accepted and valued by Him, and so that we could learn we have a place at His table. Ephesians 1:6, KJV tells us we are "accepted in the beloved." The Lord welcomes us into His family through His Son Jesus. All who accept Jesus are called "children of God" (John 1:12, NASB). One day, Jesus will bring everyone in the family to the dinner table together at the "marriage supper of the Lamb" (Revelation 19:9, NASB). Meals are such a sweet place of fellowship. Delicious dishes, captivating conversation, and the presence of loved ones make for precious memories. The Lord knows these things, and we get to experience a glimpse of the fellowship He intends for us in heaven when we gather around the table on earth. Patrick got to experience that beautiful picture when he was invited to the lunch table at school.

I know about being invited to the table. Shortly after David and I began visiting First Baptist Church with our family, we decided to attend a special Sunday Night Supper and Bible Study the church was hosting. The late arrival of our babysitter set us up to arrive after the gathering had started. When we walked in the door, awkwardness pressed upon me as I realized everyone was seated, dinner was nearly over, and the study was about to begin. The crowded room made it difficult to locate any vacant seats. Furthermore, I realized this wasn't the casual gathering I thought it would be. Everyone was nicely dressed, and here David and I were in blue jeans. I felt completely vulnerable and out of place.

Suddenly, Faye Bragg, a senior member of the congregation, was at our side. I remembered her from the Sunday School class we had just visited.

"Hello, dear ones," she said. "Let me get you some supper, and you can sit with me at our table."

She took us to the kitchen window and asked the kitchen workers for two extra plates, all the while smiling and making pleasant conversation with David and me.

"How are those precious children of yours? Who is watching them tonight? We sure are glad you could join us this evening," she said.

By the time she deposited us at her table and retrieved our Bible study materials, I felt completely at ease and welcomed.

I have never forgotten that experience. I often ask the Lord to make me aware of people who are new or visiting my church or the different groups I belong to. I hope the Lord will use me to let them know they are welcome at the table. He has welcomed me, so I want to be part of welcoming others.

Socially, Patrick has faced a marathon of challenges in relating to people. Engaging in conversations and expressing friendship have never come easily for him. In grade school, he made two close friends: Alex Pinion and Angel Garcia. All three boys shared a love of video games and would gather to play the games, watch videos, and discuss the gaming industry. Alex especially liked to take a big brother role with Patrick at school, teaching him the ropes and encouraging him to succeed academically and socially.

When middle school came around, Patrick and Alex headed to China Grove Middle School, while Angel attended nearby Southeast Middle School. Although Patrick and Alex were at the same school, they were on different "teams," so they did not have any classes together. Alex couldn't look out for Patrick like he used to, and Patrick definitely felt the void in his friendship. Like a river being fed by several tributaries, the middle school received students from three local elementary schools. Many of the students there did not know Patrick. For all my children, I have found the middle school years to be most trying. It seems as if the young people there are trying to "find their place in the pack," and a lot of jockeying happens as each child tries to secure his or her position in the school community. Patrick struggled with coolness and conformity, and as a result, became the target of bullying shortly after entering sixth grade.

He told me about being pushed and shoved in the hallways, about being called "fatso" and "retard," and about certain guys waiting for him in the stairwell who would knock his books out of his hands or take his lunch or his jacket.

I called the school after each incident, and they promised to try to monitor the situation.

Patrick and I talked and prayed about the bullying, about how to handle it, about what to say and do, and about how to try to protect himself from it.

"It's wrong! It is not acceptable!" I reminded Patrick. "You need to tell someone in the guidance office when it happens. Avoid the stairwells when you are alone. And pray! Pray for the bullies, because they must have a lot of pain in their lives to be acting that way. Ask God to help them know how much He loves them, and to heal them of their hurts, and the hurt they are causing others."

We continually talked about these things. The bullying kept us on our knees in prayer.

***

"Patrick has experienced a rather severe bullying incident, and we need you to come to the school," the guidance counselor said.

"Is he okay?" I asked fearfully.

I was out running errands when I answered my cellphone.

"He's okay. We have him in the office. He is pretty shaken up, but he's okay. We asked him if he wanted us to call you, and he said yes," she replied.

I was already turning the van around toward the school.

"I'll be there in 15 minutes," I assured her.

When I walked into the counselor's office, I found Patrick, hunched in a corner chair vigorously squeezing a stress ball. His face was flushed, and his eyes were red and swollen from a deluge of tears.

"Can I give you a hug, Patrick?" I whispered.

He nodded.

"What happened?" I asked, turning to the counselor.

"From what we can gather, a student assaulted Patrick in the boys' locker room as they were changing out for P.E. The student was making fun of Patrick and then shoved him into the lockers," she said.

"He was making fun of the kind of underwear I wore," Patrick offered, amid sniffles.

Seriously?! I thought, anger building. *Underwear? You're going to beat someone up over underwear?!*

"We don't know the identity of the student because Patrick can't remember his name," the counselor said.

"Where was the PE teacher?" I asked, knowing the school required locker room supervision during classes.

"We are looking into that. He should have been in there when everything happened, but he wasn't," the counselor said.

I turned to Patrick. He was my main concern at this point.

"Do you want to go home?" I asked.

"Yes," he said.

We gathered up his stuff and went to the van.

Lord, I can't make any sense of this. It's just pure evil to me. Please protect Patrick, and don't let his spirit get crushed under the weight of this meanness, I prayed.

Later that afternoon, I received another phone call. It was from the mother of another student in the PE class.

"My son was really concerned about what happened to Patrick today. Is he okay? My son insisted that I call and check on him. I'm not trying to be nosy; we genuinely care about Patrick," she said. "And, my son wants to give you the name of the boy who bullied Patrick. He knows his name."

My heart melted at the kindness of this family, and at the risk this boy was taking in exposing the bully. I knew how angry, aggressive, and hurt individuals could retaliate against others.

"Thank you so much," I said. "Please tell your son that Patrick is improving, and he will feel even better when he hears that your son asked you to call."

I called the school guidance office and gave them the name of the bully. I knew this young man needed some help in overcoming his hostile and overly aggressive tendencies. I prayed the school would be able to help him with his struggles.

"Patrick, do you see how people care about you? This mother and her son called to check on you, and they gave us some information that will help," I said.

I could see the encouragement Patrick found in my words. Juxtaposed against the stone-hard cruelty of the day's events were the compassion and courage of a mother and son, who were determined to help someone being abused. We never had to deal with that bully again.

When Patrick entered high school, his social relationships took another hit. His friend Angel's family moved to Gastonia, about an hour's drive away. He wouldn't be in town any more to visit and hang out. His friend Alex moved to the newly opened Carson High School, so he would not be at school with Patrick either.

"I won't have any friends at school," Patrick groaned. "And it is so hard for me to make friends."

I watched as he tried to invite friends over, only to have them make repeated excuses as to why they could not come. Once, he planned a party for seven friends, and, one by one, each one of them cancelled.

But he did not give up. He kept inviting people. He kept calling. Eventually, people started accepting his invitations, and he developed some close friendships with members of the chorus and swim team at South Rowan. By the time he was a senior, he had people inviting him to their houses.

Outward appearances can be deceiving. Cliques and social groups can be barriers more than bridges. Patrick has no clue about these things. He welcomes and remains open to everyone. He sees worth in every person, because each one is a person, uniquely crafted by God. I have gone to school events with him and have watched him greet and be greeted by girls dressed in cheerleading outfits and young men dressed in chains and black leather. I've seen him converse with members of the National Honor Society and the Future Farmers of America. He doesn't categorize people. He looks past the exterior and looks into the windows of their souls and says, "Hey, I think you're someone worth knowing."

God does that. He knows each of us at the deepest level. He knows the good and the bad, and He says, "Hey, I think you're someone worth dying for." And He did. He is always looking out for us, knowing everything wonderful He has put in us and has made available for us. He is the "God who sees" everything pertaining to our lives (Gen. 16:13, NASB), and who loves us in the very midst of it all. Patrick gave me a little glimpse of how God looks at people. We are so blessed to be ever under His watchful gaze!

Patrick's Perspective:

I am grateful for all the people who have reached out to me, and it makes me want to reach out to others. I am in college now, and I really try to talk with and include people there. I especially want to make the incoming freshmen feel more welcome. On the Pfeiffer swim team, the girls hang out together, and the boys socialize with themselves. I am talking with the team leaders about ways we can help both groups interact more and do stuff as a team. It is a blessing to get to know others.

Teachers and my parents have helped me over the years by trying to teach me the social rules of life—how you should treat people and interact with them, how to make a friend and be a friend. I appreciate this help. I really appreciate a friend when I have one, and I care about being a good friend to others. George Moreno was like a big brother and best friend to me when I joined the swim team at Pfeiffer University. His friendship helped me successfully settle into college life. He graduated after my freshman year. I hope I can be like George to the new freshmen who will join the swim team. I want to be a good leader and friend because I know how those qualities impacted my life through George.

SOMETHING TO THINK ABOUT:

Have you ever been "welcomed to the table"?

Say a prayer of thanksgiving for that experience.

Whom can you "welcome to the table" in your

places of activity and influence?

Would you ask the Lord to open your eyes to people who

need to know about His acceptance and love?

*Patrick and Alex hamming it up after one of
Patrick's chorus madrigal dinners*

Patrick and Jeremiah also sang together in Chorus

Caleb, Kristina, and Patrick heading to prom

*Patrick sporting his tuxedo before
joining friends to go to prom*

SUSAN JANE KING

21

DRIVING

"Behold, I will do something new, now it will spring forth;
Will you not be aware of it?
I will even make a roadway in the wilderness,
rivers in the desert."
—Isaiah 43:19, NASB

Click-click. Click-click. Click-click.

The turn signal pulsed as Patrick cautiously turned the steering wheel and navigated our little Honda Civic around the empty parking lot at South Rowan High School.

It was about our 40th turn that afternoon! I kept my eyes straight ahead so the usual car sickness wouldn't set in.

"Good job, Patrick. You're doing great," I said.

Patrick passed his driver's education class when he was 15, but he had resisted driving for years.

"I'm afraid to drive, Mom," he had told me. "Everything comes at you so fast, and there is too much to keep up with—watching your mirrors, checking your speed, following all the rules of driving, and paying attention to others drivers and everything around the road—it is overwhelming to me!"

I didn't push him. I knew he would let me know when he was ready to drive.

Three years later, he came home from school one day and said, "Mom, I am thinking it is time for me to get my driver's license."

I looked at him with surprise, and said, "Really? What made you decide that?"

"All my friends are driving, and I am not. I have to get a ride everywhere I go. I want to be able to do what my friends are doing. I am starting to be embarrassed that I don't have a license," Patrick said.

"Well, I think it's a great idea for you to get your license!" I said. "And I know you can do it! I am proud of you for overcoming your fears."

"Oh, I am still afraid to do it," Patrick said, "but sometimes, you have to face your fears because it is the right thing to do—and now the right thing to do is to learn how to drive."

Admiration for my son's courage filled my heart.

I had seen a television interview of Temple Grandin, who has autism and serves as a strong advocate and spokesperson for individuals with autism. She talked about teaching an autistic person to drive.

"It is all about muscle memory," she had said. "Let them practice making turns, using the brakes, accelerating with the gas pedal, looking in the mirrors, turning the steering wheel—all the mechanics of driving—in a safe place, until the patterns of the movements get wired into their brains. Take as long as they need, and do it over and over."[xi]

That's why we were here in the parking lot of South Rowan High School on that breezy winter day, practicing all of those elements repeatedly. We had established a routine for Patrick, going through the driving drills three days a week (he chose the days) for nearly three months now.

"How about if we go out of the parking lot today onto the main road and then pull back in on the other school driveway?" I asked.

"You mean where the cars drive?!" Patrick asked in alarm.

"Yep. I think you are ready to do that," I said.

Patrick nervously steered our iron carriage onto the main road, went about 500 feet, then hit his turn signal and zipped the car back into the parking lot.

"You did it!" I exclaimed.

He smiled, pleased with this minor triumph.

Over the next few months, I convinced him to venture out even farther, going to the stop sign at the end of the street and then returning to the school, turning right at the stop sign and going down the road to the local Y and then returning to the school, steering down the main road back to our house, and eventually driving around the country roads that blanketed our community.

His autistic traits helped him in that he knew all the driving rules and strictly adhered to them. And his autistic traits *challenged* him in that he knew all the driving rules and strictly adhered to them!

"Patrick, you need to be looking at the road and your mirrors more than you are looking at the speedometer," I said.

"But, I am one mile over the speed limit!" he said. "I don't want to get a ticket!"

"You are not going to get a ticket for going one mile over the speed limit," I replied.

"But the rule is 35 miles per hour," Patrick said adamantly. "Not 36."

"You are not going to get a ticket for going one mile over the speed limit," I repeated. "Trust me. It's okay. Just try to stay close to the posted speed. Nobody can drive the speed limit perfectly all the time."

Despite my urgings, Patrick struggled for months with his obsession to drive the exact speed limit. He nearly panicked when the speedometer wand drifted off the magic number. Eventually, however, after months of driving practice, the urgency of precisely satisfying the speed limit lost its hold on him.

But he still stuck to the other driving rules like glue.

"Ugh! It is so annoying riding with Patrick," Sarah said one day, after returning from a car trip with him.

"Why?" I asked.

"Well, I got in the front seat with him, and he told me I needed to put on my seatbelt," Sarah said.

"I'm with Patrick. You should wear your seatbelt," I said.

"Well, I told Patrick I didn't want to wear it!" Sarah said. "And do you know what he did?!"

"What?" I said.

"He told me, 'We learned in driver's education Sarah that statistically, your chance of being seriously injured or dying in a car accident goes up 50 percent if you are not wearing your seatbelt. So I am not going to start the car until you put your seatbelt on.'

Then, he just sat there with his hands folded in his lap looking at me!"

"What did you do?" I asked.

"I put on my seatbelt," Sarah said, exasperated.

Thank You for Patrick's adherence to the rules, Lord, I prayed with amusement.

When the time came for Patrick to take his driving test, I contacted his friend Kristina and asked her what the examination was like so I could prepare Patrick in advance. She provided me with a detailed description of the roads they drove, the instructions the examiner gave, and the challenges along the route. Patrick and I drove the course 10 times, practicing the maneuvers Kristina mentioned, before he went to take his test.

Test day dawned bright and promising. Patrick's cheerful disposition matched the spring-like weather outside. The many months of practice had established a strong confidence for the task at hand. He waved goodbye, smiling as he left the driver's license building with the examiner. We had prayed in the car before we entered the building, but I prayed again at that moment.

Lord, help him do well on his driver's test. Help him remember everything he has practiced. Incline the examiner's heart toward him, and grant him success. Thank You for being with him today—and every day he is driving.

Patrick reentered the building about 20 minutes later and shot me a thumbs-up, accompanied by a huge smile.

"I passed!" he exclaimed.

"Awesome! I am so proud of you!" I said, shooting back a thumbs-up of my own.

Patrick embraced the newfound freedom his driver's license gave him. He relished being able to drive himself to swim practices, enjoying his new capability to choose when he would leave and return home, instead of waiting on others to ferry him around.

He also learned that other drivers don't always behave properly.

"Mom!" he called, coming through the door. "A car stayed on my bumper all the way home from school today! And I was going the speed limit. Why did they do that?!"

"Some people just get impatient," I said. "Don't let that affect you and make you break the law."

"I won't," Patrick said, "but I just don't understand why

people don't do what they are supposed to do."

That's a good question, I thought.

Over time, Patrick branched out more and more with his driving, testing his skills on the interstate, in varying weather conditions, and for longer distances. Eventually, his driving abilities opened the door for him to swim on a club swim team in Misenheimer, NC, before he started his freshman year in college. He faithfully embarked in the Civic every day, Monday through Friday, and made the 60-minute round trip to the Nomad practice on his own.

Honestly, David and I had wondered if Patrick would ever drive a car in the early days of his autism diagnosis. Today, we consider him to be one of the best drivers in the family. He pays close attention to everything around him when he is driving, and he follows the rules. Even when other people don't do what they are supposed to be doing!

Patrick's Perspective:

Driving truly was a challenge for me in the beginning, especially since people can be unpredictable and do not follow the rules all the time. One time, when I was driving home from school, a car passed me when there was a solid double yellow line on the road—and it was a mother with her child! I could not believe that mom would put her and her child's life at risk because she was in such a hurry! I hope people will be careful on the roads, because driving is a big responsibility. I know when I start my car that my decisions can affect others and me. That is why I try to be careful.

I remember being overly focused on the speed limit for a long time. I even tried to go 5 or 10 miles below the speed limit, just to be safe. My parents quickly convinced me that I could make some enemies on the road that way! After driving a while, I realized I needed to mostly be aware of and adjust to the traffic conditions around me. I think life is like that. You can have a general plan and guidelines for your life, but you have to be flexible, too, adjusting to what comes along your way. And I am still cautious on the road and try to follow the rules.

SOMETHING TO THINK ABOUT:

What is something new the Lord might be doing in your life?

Would you trust Him and move forward with Him?

How has the Lord opened up new things for you?

Take some time to thank Him for those things today.

How have you had to adjust to the "road conditions"

around you? Would you be flexible, responding to

what the Lord has for you today?

Patrick . . . driving!

22

LEAVING YOUR PROBLEMS
AT THE DOOR

*"Cast all your anxiety on Him
because He cares for you."*
—*1 Peter 5:7, NIV*

Patrick's friend Lindsay was headed into the chorus room for
Varsity Singers class when she noticed Patrick, hunched against the
wall outside the door, with a pained look on his face.

"Patrick? Why aren't you going into class? It's almost time to
start," Lindsay said.

Patrick looked up at Lindsay, president of the Varsity Singers,
an inspiring leader, who had told them at the start of the year to
leave their problems at the door before coming into class each day.

"I am having trouble leaving my problems at the door,"
Patrick said.

Lindsay had instructed him to leave his problems at the door,
so he was not going to set foot into the room until he had
deposited his troubles outside, at the doorframe. A difficult task on
that particular day.

"What's wrong?" Lindsay asked.

Patrick bared his soul about the test gone wrong, the
misunderstanding with friends, and the challenges of learning
complicated class material.

Lindsay listened with a sympathetic ear.

"She encouraged me a lot after I talked to her, and then I

could go through the door," Patrick told me later.

My heart warmed, and I chuckled as I pictured that interchange outside the chorus classroom—Patrick's literalness at its finest!

Anxiety often assaults autistic individuals. With all their challenges and struggles, fears and worries can come in rapid progression. Stress, as Patrick called it, would make him feel pressure in his chest and nervousness throughout his body.

I am grateful Patrick would always tell me when he was dealing with anxiety. We would talk through his problems and take them to the Lord in prayer. I could visibly see his body and face relax when we prayed—because Patrick trusts God. I guess that's why the Bible says God is "the help of my countenance (face)" (Psalm 42:11, NASB). Our relationship with Him can literally show itself in our faces!

I remember reading 1 Peter 5:7, NIV, where it said, "Cast all your anxiety on Him because He cares for you," and looking up that word "anxiety" in my Bible concordance. I was surprised to see it meant "(through the idea of distraction) solicitude."[xii] I realized that the fears and anxieties I experienced were actually an attempt to draw my eyes, ears, and heart away from the Lord to focus on something else. Then I looked up the word "cares," and I caught my breath. It means "to be of interest and concern to, to be an object of care."[xiii] It carries the idea that the Lord has His eyes on me. So I do not need to be distracted by the stuff going on around me because the Lord is totally focused on me. He is over everything concerning me. He loves me. And He will accomplish His purpose for me. Now, when worries, anxieties, and fears assail me, I try to remember to view them as a reminder to choose to trust, thank, and praise the Lord. I can "draw near with confidence to the throne of grace" (Hebrews 4:16, NASB) and leave my problems at the door.

Patrick's Perspective:

It took me a while even to figure out the clues to when I was getting stressed. Lots of people have helped me with this. When I was in high school, I went back to the TEACCH Center, and Sue McCarter helped me figure out how my body reacted to stress, and she taught me relaxation techniques. My teachers and the counselors at school are always available to talk with me. When I need time to myself at home, I put a sign on the door to the basement (where my bedroom is located). The sign says, "Patrick in residence." It lets my family know I need some space.

Another blessing in handling the stress is my faith. When I feel stressed, I pray, and it settles my spirit because I know that God cares about me and that He has a plan for my life. My family helps me with the stress, too. They help me sort things out, and their love and support keep me going.

SOMETHING TO THINK ABOUT:

What makes you anxious, worried, or fearful?

What persons or things try to distract you from

your fellowship with the Lord?

Would you look at the Lord instead of your problems today

and choose to trust, thank, and praise Him?

As you go into the doorway where you will spend

most of your day today, try uttering a prayer to the Lord,

releasing your anxieties to Him, and embracing

His presence and provision.

23

ENTERING THE PUBLIC FORUM

*"My mouth will speak the praise of the Lord,
and all flesh will bless His holy name forever and ever."*
—*Psalm 145:21, NASB*

As time passed, the Lord began putting Patrick and me in front of audiences so that others might hear about the joy and purpose He can give in the midst of living with autism.

In May 2012, we were asked to serve as the keynote speakers at a Special Needs Mini-Conference held on the campus of Catawba College in Salisbury, NC. Our talk was entitled, "The Challenges and Blessings of Living with Autism." Patrick and I shared what it was like to live with autism and the many lessons the Lord taught us along the way. Our presentation can be viewed on YouTube. (See link at the back of this book.)

I watched parents, educators, and support persons shed many tears as they empathized and gained insights and hope regarding the world of autism. As I scanned the faces of the many young mothers in the auditorium, I remembered being in their shoes so many years before. My heart went out to them.

Thank You, Lord, for allowing us to be here so these women can know there is always hope with You, I prayed.

At the end of his talk, Patrick sang "Thankful," by Josh Groban, "because that's what I am," he said.

Norma Honeycutt, the facilitator of the event, asked afterward, "Please stand if you saw your child in Patrick today."

Nearly the entire auditorium stood up.

"Thank you, Patrick, for giving a voice to our children," she said.

Patrick nodded and smiled.

Yes, he has given a voice to those with autism. A beautiful, encouraging voice. In truth, his voice simply reflects the voice of a loving Father in heaven, who says, "Nothing is impossible with God" (Luke 1:37, NASB).

As his high school graduation neared, Brian Farmer, the youth pastor at our church, asked Patrick if he would give the sermon on Graduation/Youth Sunday.

"I will need to pray about it and see if God wants me to do it," Patrick replied.

A few weeks later, Patrick told Brian, "God says I should do it."

None of us was prepared for what the Lord did on that Sunday. Patrick stood in front of a packed church and spoke about his experiences with his autism and the lessons the Lord had taught him through it. Church members dabbed tears as Patrick shared from his heart.

"For years, I thought of myself as the boy with autism. That was my identity," Patrick said. "But my identity is not that I am the boy with autism. My identity is that I am the boy who Jesus loves."

I thought back to my prayers so many years ago. The Lord had helped Patrick realize that He loved him, and He had made him strong in light of that love. And he was ready to tell the world about it.

Since he spoke at our church, Patrick has been asked to share at other churches in our community. His inspiring story has blessed many individuals.

Patrick's graduation sermon was entitled, "Identity and Integrity in Christ," and can be found on YouTube. (See link at the back of this book.)

At the end of his sermon, he said, "And now, I would like to share a song with you. It is called 'Forevermore,' by Travis Cottrell![xiv] This song means a lot to me because it tells about who God is to me, who He is to all of us." That song is based on Psalm 145, which says,

I will exalt You, my God the King; I will praise Your name for

ever and ever. Every day I will praise You and extol Your name for ever and ever. Great is the Lord and most worthy of praise; His greatness no one can fathom. One generation commends Your works to another; they tell of Your mighty acts. They speak of the glorious splendor of Your majesty—and I will meditate on Your wonderful works.They tell of the power of Your awesome works—and I will proclaim Your great deeds. They celebrate Your abundant goodness and joyfully sing of Your righteousness. The Lord is gracious and compassionate, slow to anger and rich in love. The Lord is good to all; He has compassion on all He has made. All Your works praise You, Lord; Your faithful people extol You. They tell of the glory of Your kingdom and speak of Your might so that all people may know of Your mighty acts and the glorious splendor of Your kingdom. Your kingdom is an everlasting kingdom, and Your dominion endures through all generations. The Lord is trustworthy in all He promises and faithful in all He does. My mouth will speak in praise of the Lord. Let every creature praise His holy name for ever and ever. —Psalm 145:1-13, 21, NIV

So be it. Amen.

Patrick's Perspective:

Before I started speaking in public, I was really nervous to speak in front of people. But every time I have spoken about my autism and what the Lord has done, I felt His presence with me, and I knew He was going to do amazing things. So I was not afraid when I began speaking. I just gave it to the Lord, and it became His work. I feel happy to share my story with others and to help encourage them through my experiences and challenges. I could not talk, and now I get to tell people about Jesus!

SOMETHING TO THINK ABOUT:

How might the Lord want to use you

to praise His name?

Would you look for opportunities—in what you say

and in what you do—to praise God every day?

What has God done in your life?

How can you tell others about it?

SUSAN JANE KING

24

WALKING THROUGH THE OPEN DOOR

*"Behold, I have put before you an open door
which no one can shut."*
—*Revelation 3:8, NASB*

"**M**om, I'm nervous," Patrick said.

"What are you nervous about?" I asked.

"The interview. You know how long it takes me to put my thoughts together to answer a question. It takes me a while to figure out what to say," Patrick said.

He was getting ready to go to the interview portion of Accepted Students Day at Pfeiffer University, an interview which would decide whether or not he would receive additional scholarship money.

"Could you just tell the people interviewing you that you have autism so it takes you a while to pull your thoughts together?" I suggested. "It might be good for them to know and learn a little about autism."

"Yeah. I guess I could do that," Patrick said.

He looked handsome in his khaki pants, blue shirt, and yellow and blue striped tie. His navy blue jacket made him look much older than he was. He looked like a young man before me.

"How do I look?" he asked.

"Like a scholarship winner," I said with a wink.

He laughed.

"I hope the interview committee thinks so," he said.

"Could you pray for me?" Patrick asked as we pulled into the visitor parking space at Pfeiffer.

"Sure," David said. "Let's huddle up."

We stood in a circle beside our blue Honda Odyssey van. David stretched his strong arms around Patrick and me and began to pray.

"Lord, we know You have brought us here to this place, and we know You are with Patrick and will go with him into his interview today. Give him peace. Let him sense Your presence with him. Let him have fun, and let him bless the interviewers. Give Patrick the words to share with them. We trust You with the process and the outcome. Thank You for this wonderful opportunity and for all Your many blessings. Amen."

"Amen," Patrick said.

We walked over to the chapel and listened to a presentation about the university. Then, Patrick left with a group of students for his interview. The university representatives told us his interview should last 10 to 15 minutes. After 40 minutes, I turned to David and said, "I wonder why it is taking so long. We did tell Patrick to meet us back here at the chapel, right?"

"Yes we did," he said. "Give it a little more time."

Another five minutes rolled by.

"Can we just go over to the building where they are interviewing and make sure he is still there?" I asked. Visions of Patrick wandering all over campus looking for us filled my mind.

Maybe he had forgotten how to find his way back to the chapel. He had only been to the campus one other time.

"Okay. Let's go see what we can find out," David said.

When we entered Jane Freeman Hall, one of the admissions counselors came up to us and said, "They must really be enjoying their interview with Patrick. They have had him in there for 45 minutes."

Whoa, I thought. *That's a long time for him to talk! I hope it's going okay.*

"Here he comes now," she said.

Patrick was striding down the hall, beaming from ear to ear.

"How did it go?" I asked.

"Great!" he said. "I liked them. They were really nice, and they were very interested in what I had to say."

"How many people were in the room?" I asked.

"Three," he said.

"What did they ask you?" David asked.

"Well, they asked me what was the greatest challenge I had to face in life and how did I handle it?" he said.

"What did you say?" I asked.

"I told them it definitely was my autism, and how I handled it was I asked God to help me, and He did," Patrick said.

I knew those interviewers didn't hear that kind of answer very often. I rejoiced, knowing they could see that Patrick's response was genuine. He relied on the Lord, day in and day out. His "weakness" had caused him to look to God for strength, and it had grown his faith in miraculous ways.

"Wow! That's a great answer! I am so proud of you," I said. "What else did they ask you?"

"They wanted to know if I could talk with anyone in the past or in the present, who would it be and why," Patrick said.

"That's a great question," David said. "Whom did you choose?"

"Well, I told them I would like to talk with Walt Disney because he was so creative, and I would like to know where he got his creative ideas from," said Patrick.

"That's good!" David said.

"Then, they said, tell us someone else," Patrick added, "so I said Albert Einstein, because they think he had autism, and he was pretty successful, so I would like to know if he had any advice for me on how to be successful since I have autism too."

"Wow!" David said.

"One of the interviewers said, 'Yeah, he was *pretty* successful,'" Patrick said, grinning.

"Then, they said, give us another!" Patrick said. "So I told them Temple Grandin, and guess what? They had never heard of her! So I got to tell them all about her."

One of our heroines on the autism spectrum, Temple Grandin is an accomplished author and speaker, who holds a PhD, and who advocates for understanding and acceptance of autistic individuals. The movie, *The Temple Grandin Story* is one of Patrick's favorites. She has made great inroads in helping others understand what it is like to be autistic.

"Did they ask you anything about swimming?" David asked.

"Well, one of them asked me about my swimming, and I told them I was going to swim on the Pfeiffer swim team. Then one said, 'So you must be pretty good at swimming?'"

"What did you say to that?" David asked.

"I told him, 'not yet,'" Patrick said.

"That's perfect, Bub, because it shows you think you can get better and want to!" David said.

"Well, both of those are true," Patrick said.

"Did they ask you about what you want to study and what you want to do someday for work?" I asked.

"Yes, and what's really cool is that one of the guys in there really likes video games, and we got to talk a lot about them. It was fun," Patrick said.

"It was fun." That was exactly what David had prayed for in his prayer . . . that and the score of other things that happened in an amazing span of 45 minutes. I silently thanked God for giving Patrick the opportunity to be understood, accepted, and valued for the unique young man he was.

When we got back in the van, David said another prayer thanking God for answering all the requests of his earlier prayer and for making His presence felt during the interview.

Two weeks later, we received a phone call from the Admissions Department, telling us that Patrick was being awarded the Stokes Scholarship based on his outstanding interview results.

Look at what You did, Lord! I exclaimed as I hung up the phone. *Patrick, who struggles with relating to people and knowing what to say, just won a scholarship based on his interaction and communication with a group of professionals he didn't even know! Your wonders never cease!*

As I reflected on the interview experience, I remembered how nervous I had been for Patrick. But in the end, he enjoyed and even benefitted from his session with the interviewers. It made me realize that when I face uncomfortable and challenging situations, they can never stand in my way if God is with me. Whenever He opens a door, no one can close it. And He had just flung the door to Pfeiffer University wide open.

Patrick's Perspective:

One of the scholarship interviewers was Dr. Ali Sever, chair of the Computer Information Systems Department. We formed a friendship that day that continues. God taught me through that interview experience that He gives me the words I need to speak, and He goes with me into every situation. I never have to be afraid because He is with me. And if He takes me into an uncomfortable situation, He has a blessing for me in it. I could tell God was working through me because I felt strong and confident in my answers, which was really unusual for me.

SOMETHING TO THINK ABOUT:

What uncomfortable or challenging

situation are you facing right now?

Make a list of some of the "obstacles" you perceive

in your life. Would you commit them to God, realizing

that He can make a way in any circumstance?

Would you allow the Lord to bless you through the

uncomfortable situations you face?

25

STARTING COLLEGE

*"You will keep in perfect peace all who trust in You,
all whose thoughts are fixed on You!"*
—Isaiah 26:3, NLT

I felt the lump rising in my throat, and I pushed it down again. I was neatly placing T-shirts into the chest of drawers in Patrick's dorm room. Moving-in day. It came faster than I thought it would. I didn't have a good track record on these days: 0 for 3. I had broken down every time I had dropped a child off at college. Thankfully, when I took Katie to UNC-Charlotte, it was dark outside when we said goodbye, and she didn't have to see my tears. With Emily, her Dad and I walked her to the cafeteria at East Carolina University after we had set up her dorm room. I quickly hugged her, turned, and started marching to the car as the cascade of tears hit. I planned the same exit strategy with Sarah, but she ran after me for one last hug, and I could not hold back the sobs. And here I was with Patrick, my autistic, special-needs son, and I was about to leave him adrift in the sea of the unknown with no routines, no predictability yet in place. I shuddered at the thought.

Pound. Pound. Pound.

Wielding a hammer, David was busy lofting Patrick's bed and setting up his desk underneath.

I smiled.

David often showed love through acts of service for others. Here he was, creating the "super dorm room" for Patrick. I admired him so.

After several hours, it was time to leave.

"I've got to go to an orientation meeting," Patrick said, looking at the schedule in his hands. "I don't want to be late."

Patrick was all about following schedules and doing what he was supposed to do. It made his world manageable.

We walked outside to our van.

"Goodbye," Patrick said. He hugged each of us and hurried off to his meeting.

"He doesn't even feel bad about us leaving," David said. "That's so good!"

I looked at him in shock.

"Don't you see? He's already jumped into his life here. He's looking forward, not back," David said.

Joy intermingled with the sorrow and fear in my heart. David was right. That was a good sign. I wiped a few tears as we drove home, but I was hopeful. Hopeful that Patrick might actually be able to adjust to college. Hopeful that the people at Pfeiffer University might embrace him just as he was trying to embrace them. Hopeful that he might get the education and experience he needed to secure a rewarding job someday.

Lord, thank You for bringing Patrick to Pfeiffer, I prayed. *I know You have great plans for him there, for him to be blessed and for him to be a blessing to others. I know I won't be with him every day anymore, and I am really going to miss him. Please help me with that. And even though I won't be with him, I know You will be. Thank You for taking care of him and for helping him adjust to college. Thank You for using him to let others know how wonderful You are.*

Peace filled my heart as we drove home.

Several weeks before, the reality of Patrick's imminent departure for college had hit me. I had asked the Lord to help me as I struggled with fear about his future. One day, as I walked back into the house after visiting the grocery store, I heard music playing in the kitchen. The CD player was running, but nobody was home.

My eyes brimmed with tears as I soaked in the Lord's kindness. The Casting Crowns song "Already There"[xv] reminded me to redirect my thoughts to the Lord's faithfulness and His perfect plans for Patrick's life, that the Lord had gone ahead of Patrick to Pfeiffer and had made a path for him there, a path that led to a God-ordained future, full of hope, promise, and purpose.

Once again, I had to choose to trust the Lord and release my son to Him. I had to trust the same Lord who had been so faithful with Patrick in the past to take care of him in the future. I knew I had to remember and think about the Lord instead of the uncertain road ahead. And He helped me to do just that.

The day I left Patrick at college and drove home with David, I had to choose to trust the Lord again. Many times through that first year on campus, I had to choose faith over fear. Peace comes when I remember who God is . . . everything else pales in comparison. I heard someone say once that we can trust an unknown future to a known God. It's true. Because He is already there.

Patrick's Perspective:

Even though I was trying to follow the schedule on the day my parents left me at college, I still really missed them. I almost cried the first night I was all alone in my dorm room. But I trusted the Lord that He would provide the help I needed and the friends I needed in college. And sure enough, He did!

Dr. Jim Gulledge, director of Academic Support Services, helped me with the accommodations I needed, like extended time on tests. He also helped me get a private dorm room so I would have a place to go and decompress all by myself. Dr. Ali Sever, my adviser, professor, and chair of the Computer Information Systems Department, helped me organize the classes I needed to take for my major. I could meet with either of these two people whenever I needed them.

My professors were very helpful, too, and encouraged me a lot. The Pfeiffer swim team became like a family to me, and I made close friends there. Coach Anderson encouraged me when I felt like I was not contributing enough to the team. He said all he wanted was my very best, and I worked hard to give it to him. Even though I had stressful moments in college, I could relieve that stress by getting together with my friends, especially George, Zach, Luke, and Henry.

SOMETHING TO THINK ABOUT:

What frightens you about the future?

What uncertainties are you facing?

What do you know about the Lord that

would address those fears?

Say a prayer of thanks to the Lord that He

holds the future in His hands.

Patrick showing off his freshman-year dorm room

Patrick settled into campus life at Pfeiffer University

Patrick quickly found his way around campus at Pfeiffer

*Patrick at the pedestal clock, located at the
heart of Pfeiffer's campus*

Patrick and Pfeiffer were a good match

Patrick at his home away from home—
the computer lab at Pfeiffer University

26

BEING SHARPENED AS SIBLINGS

"Iron sharpens iron;
so a man sharpens the countenance of his friend
[to show rage or worthy purpose]."
—Proverbs 27:17, Amp.

When difficulties come crashing into our lives, we all have the choice either to be angry, and rage about it, or to look for and embrace God's purpose in it. We often cannot control what happens to us in life, but we can control how we react to it. We can be sharpened toward anger or purpose. I have seen those principles at work in my own family.

Often, I felt bad for my daughters, who had to experience the challenges and demands of living with an autistic brother. Now, I'm glad they did. Because I have seen the way Patrick's life has shaped them to be caring, sensitive young women who have a passion for the handicapped.

Sure, it has been crazy at times. Like when Katie had the sleepover of her 8-year-old friends, and Patrick, age 2, walked into the room completely naked because he was going through a phase where he didn't like the feeling of clothes on his body. (He would strip every chance he got.) We stayed home a lot during that phase! Relatively shy, Emily would get annoyed and embarrassed every time we were out in public and Patrick drew attention to us through his noises and repetitive behaviors. Sarah had to go through two years of high school with Patrick in tow.

"I'm so embarrassed!" Sarah announced, marching into the house one day after swim practice.

"What happened?" I asked.

"We were doing relay races at the pool, and Patrick got out of the lane at the end of his race and laid out on the pool deck, moaning, rolling around, and saying how hard it was!" she said.

"Well, you moan and say it's hard sometimes," I said, winking.

"Not like that!" Sarah said. "It embarrassed me in front of the team! Will you please talk to him and tell him he can't do that? I'm afraid I won't say it the right way because I'm upset."

Patrick arrived a little while later.

"How was swimming today?" I asked him.

"Okay, I guess," he said. "The relay races were really hard."

"Yeah, Sarah told me you laid out on the pool deck afterwards and were moaning about them," I said.

"Yes, because they were hard," Patrick said.

"Patrick, did you see anyone else laying down and moaning after the races?" I asked.

He paused, thinking.

"Come to think about it, no, I didn't," he said.

I could see the wheels turning in his head.

"Just so you know, people don't do that on high school teams when it is hard," I said.

"Oh no! Do you think I embarrassed Sarah?" he asked.

"That's a possibility," I said. "You might want to talk to her about it, and if you did embarrass her, you could tell her you are sorry."

"Okay. Thanks, Mom," Patrick said.

I heard him approach Sarah later that day.

"Sarah, I am really sorry if I embarrassed you by the way I behaved at the pool today," he said to his sister.

"That's okay. Just don't do it again," she said, softened by his sincerity.

"I won't," Patrick said with a pledge-type tone. "And please let me know if I am doing anything else that I shouldn't do. Would you help me with that?"

"Yes, I will," Sarah said.

That began a brother-sister alliance that exists to this day. Sarah knows how to lovingly yet firmly coach her brother on the social and other rules of life, and she displays a fierce loyalty toward him.

One day, she came home from school and slammed the door in frustration.

"I am so angry I could punch this boy at school! One of my friends told me he was making fun of Patrick at school today, and I have seen Patrick go out of his way to be nice to this guy," Sarah said. "I had to go talk to Mrs. Gore about it. This boy is in chorus with Patrick. I told Mrs. Gore she had to do something about it, or I was going to!"

"I'm sure Mrs. Gore will talk with that boy," I said. "She doesn't like to have any of that stuff happening in her chorus family."

"Well, I'm just telling you now about it, so that if I have to do something, you know about it in advance," Sarah said, her jaw set in determination.

"Sarah . . ." I started.

"Don't worry, Mom," she said. "I'm not going to do anything crazy, but I might just go off on him!"

Sarah was ready to go into battle to defend her brother. Luckily, Mrs. Gore took care of everything. But the entire incident made me smile to see how the Lord had worked in our family. We were ready to circle the wagons when a threat appeared against Patrick. I knew Sarah's fierce protection of her brother would be used to defend the weak in the future.

Sarah's experiences with Patrick gave her a tender heart and strong desire to help others. Those qualities eventually led her to pursue a bachelor of science in nursing degree. Today, as a labor and delivery and postpartum nurse, she helps mothers usher their babies into the world and learn to care for them afterwards. She loves those babies and their mothers, showering them with affection, care, and encouragement.

Katie developed a special fondness for her brother as well. Since she was 10 years old, she wanted to be a teacher; so, when she entered her senior year in high school, she signed up for an internship in a local elementary school. Much to all of our delight, she wound up interning in Patrick's fifth-grade classroom with Mrs. Dodd. During that semester, Katie and Patrick grew especially close. He insisted on sitting next to her every lunch period, and he would slip his hand in hers as they walked to her car after school every day. He became somewhat of a celebrity with his classmates, who loved Katie's passion for teaching, energetic spirit, and caring heart.

That year shaped Katie's heart to champion the disabled, handicapped, and disadvantaged students, and the Lord has brought several of those individuals into her path. She spent the next three summers as a camp counselor at Camp Seabreeze. Located in Oak Island, North Carolina, Camp Seabreeze is a Christian summer recreational program operated during daytime hours when most parents are at work. During one of Katie's summers at the camp, she met a young man named Michael. She called from camp to tell me about him.

"Mom, he reminds me so much of Patrick," she said. "He has these routines and rituals and comfort items that he has to have. I am accommodating him as best as I can. I want him to have a great camp experience!"

She shared story after story about her efforts to reach Michael. The camp was planning a talent show, an idea she had developed, and she wanted Michael to participate.

"He loves to dance, Mom. I think he should do one of his dances in the show," Katie said.

I went to the camp to watch the talent show, and in the middle of the show, Michael took the stage to dance. This blonde-haired, blue-eyed sprite gyrated all over the stage to the tune of "I like to move it, move it." When he was done, Katie's group of students jumped to their feet and erupted into applause.

"Way to go, Michael! You are awesome!" the children screamed.

A smile exploded across Michael's face.

Across the aisle from me, Michael's mother dabbed tears.

"Your attitude toward Michael made that happen," I told Katie afterward. "Your students took their lead from you and the way you have been affirming and encouraging Michael all along. I am so proud of you!"

I knew Katie's experiences with her brother had helped to shape that moment for Michael. Today, Katie is a sixth-grade teacher in a local middle school, and, not surprisingly, she serves on the team that also teaches several special needs children. Her passionate heart for the handicapped has blessed many children and families in our community.

I watched Emily over the years, too. She was the one who

wanted to "help" with Patrick. She would feed him his baby food and gently dab his mouth with a washcloth after each bite. She would help to bathe him, assist in dressing him, and sing gentle songs to him. It was no surprise to me that when he had feelings for a young lady his first year of college, he called Emily and asked her if she could give him some advice about asking a girl out on a date. My heart melted as I sat across the table from a brother and sister as they navigated that delicate subject together.

"Are you thinking you just want to be friends with this girl and hang out, or are you thinking that you might want to have her as a girlfriend?" Emily asked.

"As a girlfriend," Patrick said.

"I think that's great, Patrick. What do you like about her?" Emily said.

"I think she is as beautiful on the inside as she is on the outside," Patrick said.

"Wow! That's awesome," Emily said.

Patrick already knew this young lady. They had been playing video games together occasionally.

"Well, if you want to ask her out on a date, then what you might want to do is invite her over to the house to play video games like you usually do, and then afterward, when she is about to leave, tell her that you would like to take her on a date—use the word date—and ask her if she would like to do that," Emily said. "And then it won't have to be awkward after you ask her because she will be leaving to head home. Whatever she says, I think you are a great guy, and any girl would be lucky to have you as a boyfriend."

A sweet smile swept across Patrick's face.

"Thank you, Emily," he said.

Emily told me afterward, "I really hope she says yes!"

Patrick followed his sister's advice, but the young lady just wanted to be friends.

I watched him sob in heartache as he realized this young lady didn't feel the same way about him. As I tried to comfort him, I recognized, he really is growing up! Heartbreak over unrequited love is one of those rites of passage to adulthood. I told Patrick so. Emily was there to encourage her brother afterward as well. I was so grateful that Patrick had such supportive siblings.

Emily, too, transferred the care and empathy she developed

for Patrick over to a career in nursing. She earned a bachelor of science in nursing degree and began working right out of college as a nurse on an intensive care unit. She continues to care for acutely ill patients and their families with dedication, compassion, and excellence.

I've found that the difficult and challenging times with Patrick have helped create tender hearts in every member of our family, hearts that are open and responsive to the hurting people in the world. That's a beautiful gift from the Lord because His heart is like that, and He cares and responds to the people He has created. He loves us, and if we can love others in His name and in His way, hopefully others can get a closer look into the magnificent love He has for each one of us!

Patrick's Perspective:

It is crazy sometimes being the only guy in a family of all girls, but I am grateful for my sisters. It is hard to express how much I love my sisters. Each one of them is wonderfully unique, but what they all share in common is a loving heart. I am proud to see the young women they have become. I know God will use them to touch the lives of many others. I look up to my sisters and always will.

SOMETHING TO THINK ABOUT:

What difficult or unexpected challenge are you facing?

Will you choose to be angry about it or to look

for the Lord's worthy purpose in it?

Would you let the Lord "sharpen" you for good

through the people He puts in your life?

Patrick and Sarah, together during preschool days

Emily loved to help with Patrick

Katie exposed Patrick to many of life's adventures

*Katie, Susan, Sarah, Emily, Katie's husband Curt, David, and
Patrick, with the family dog Grace*

27

MAKING A BIG SPLASH

"No eye has seen, no ear has heard, and no mind has imagined
what God has prepared for those who love him."
—1 Corinthians 2:9, NLT

"**M**om, have you seen my Facebook page?" Patrick said.

He was calling from his dorm room at Pfeiffer University.

"No, I haven't," I said.

"Well, look at it now. I'll wait," he said.

I sat down at my computer and typed in the webpage address.

"What?! Congratulations! This is amazing!" I screamed.

Patrick had just won Pfeiffer Idol! All over his Facebook page, people were commenting and congratulating him.

"I am so proud of you!" I shouted. "Tell me all about it!"

"Well, there were about 24 of us who competed. I didn't really think I had a chance at winning because there were music majors in the contest. I just did it for fun because I haven't gotten to sing in a while, and I really am missing it," Patrick said.

"What did you have to sing? How did the competition work?" I asked.

"Well, about 24 of us each sang around two minutes of a song we picked. I sang part of 'Thankful,' by Josh Groban. Then, the judges picked four of us as finalists, and we got to sing another song for two minutes. I sang 'Forevermore,' by Travis Cottrell; then, the judges announced the winner. I can't believe I won!" he said.

"Who were the judges?" I asked.

"Professors, the Dean of Students, and stuff," Patrick said. "They were really funny. They were trying to be like the judges on American Idol! Mom, my friend George sent me some video clips from his phone. They are on my Facebook page. You should watch them."

"Okay, I will. I love you, and I am so proud of you!" I said.

Wonder took over as I hung up the phone. Wonder at the overarching goodness of the Lord, who allowed Patrick to have this experience, and amazement at how Patrick had put this entire performance together on his own and had stepped out in front of a large portion of the student body to sing. No one on the campus knew he could sing. He was about to complete his first semester as a freshman, a shy and awkward freshman who was trying to settle into campus life.

"David, you have to come watch these videos! Patrick just won Pfeiffer Idol!" I said.

David came into the room and joined me at the computer.

"What!?" he asked.

"Just watch," I said, clicking on the link.

The words to "Forevermore" floated out of our computer speakers, rich and resonant.

"Wooooooo," a scream from one of the girls watching in the campus chapel pierced the silence, and applause followed. Patrick was only nine words into his final song, and they were already cheering for him, affirming our son.

David started laughing, and I joined him. Joyous laughter. Grateful laughter. Laughter that realizes your son has been accepted and welcomed at college! Laughter that acknowledges that God is good, exceedingly good, good beyond your wildest imaginings.

The applause and shout-outs continued the entire length of Patrick's song, and at the end of it, the entire room gave him a standing ovation.

We clicked on the next video clip and watched in amazement as the announcers declared the second place winner, and the crowd began chanting, "Paddy, Paddy, Paddy" in anticipation that Patrick's name would be announced as the winner.

"They have a nickname for him," I said, grateful for the endearing words.

When the announcers called out Patrick as the winner, the entire room stood to its feet and erupted in applause. Soon, everyone was cheering, "One more song! One more song! One more song!"

"Is that really Patrick singing?" a member of the swim team had posted as a comment under the video clip on Facebook.

"Yes, it is!" George wrote.

The school newspaper later included a story about Patrick winning Pfeiffer Idol. Here are some excerpts:

"'When I saw him walk onto the stage, his smile immediately made me smile, and then he opened his mouth to sing. Goosebumps went all over my body. I kept thinking about Susan Boyle's moment on Britain's Got Talent. You would never have thought such an amazingly beautiful sound would come from Patrick, but I'm glad it did,' freshman Torri Foster said.

"'I just love him, and he is such a sweetheart!! I've known Patrick since high school, and he has always inspired me. Despite setbacks, he is still an amazing person. Nothing keeps Patrick down. He always has a contagious smile on his face, which makes my day ten times better,' freshman Katie Peeler said.

"'He should be in a Disney movie because his voice is AMAZING!' freshman Veronique Nero said."

The story also quoted Patrick. He said, "'I was happy to see people being inspired by my singing.'" The newspaper said, "King is autistic, but insists this challenge never holds him back.

"'If I can do something to make someone else happy, then I'll do it because it also makes me happy. And even if I am having a hard time, I still do the best I can,' assures King."

The story concluded by calling Patrick an "inspirational sweetheart."[xvi]

Patrick went on to win a campus coffee shop singing competition, and his dormmates convinced him to take a starring role in the Cline Hall production of the Harlem Shake. You can see it on YouTube. (See link at the back of this book.) One of his professors asked him to sing at a gathering for the Stanly Arts Council. I watched Patrick grow in confidence and in his security on campus. I knew the Lord was behind all these things.

During his spring semester freshman year, Patrick took a music theater class and was cast as Dennis Sanders in the musical "Smoke on the Mountain." We went to watch his performance and sat amazed as his velvet tenor voice produced many beautiful songs and his facial expressions and body language evoked joy and laughter from the audience. Toward the end of his freshman year, a group of friends from the swim team encouraged Patrick to participate in the Mr. Pfeiffer competition.

"What's that?" I asked him, when he told me about it.

"Well, it's a fun thing. We have to model three different outfits and compete in a talent competition," he said. "My swim team friends are helping me pick out my outfits. One of the outfits is 'Out of This World Wear.' We got a lot of tin foil for that one!"

I laughed.

"What song are you going to sing?" I asked.

"I don't know yet. I'll find something on YouTube," he said casually.

I was amazed . . . and grateful that his friends were coming around him in this endeavor.

"Mom, have you seen my Facebook page?" Patrick called and said the night of the competition.

"Did you win?!" I exclaimed.

"Yep. I did!" he said. "And a senior girl from the swim team won Miss Pfeiffer, so the swim team is going crazy right now."

I could imagine his big grin on the other end of the phone.

"Well, I've got to go because we are going out to celebrate," he said.

"Congratulations, Patrick! That is awesome! I'll tell Dad. We are both so proud of you!" I said. "Hey, by the way, what song did you sing?"

"Oh, it was a song called 'Time to Say Goodbye,' by Andrea Bocceli. I had heard it on the *Stepbrothers* movie and really liked it," he said.

Andrea Bocceli! Patrick had just sung a song by Andrea Bocceli!

David just shook his head when I told him about Patrick.

"Could he have had a better freshman year?!" he said. "He has adjusted to college life. He has made friends. He has participated on an athletic team. And he has gotten good grades."

"Thank You, Lord!" gratefully emerged from my lips.

But God's amazing work didn't end there.

Toward the end of Patrick's first semester in college, he called me with some exciting news.

"Mom, they are starting an Autism Center at Pfeiffer University, and they want me to be part of the committee that starts it!" Patrick said.

"An Autism Center? What's that?" I asked.

"They want to recruit autistic students to come to Pfeiffer, and they want to help them adjust and be successful in college. They even want to help them get jobs after college. They are planning on training teachers and parents to help autistic students, too. They said they want my help to let them know what autistic students need in college. They said they want Pfeiffer University to be the leading university for helping autistic students. And Mom, they would like for you to be part of the committee, too," Patrick said.

Suddenly, I realized the Lord had a much bigger picture in mind when He sent Patrick to Pfeiffer University. He was answering those prayers that had sprung from our hearts and mouths: that Patrick would be blessed at Pfeiffer, and that he would be a blessing to others. I knew Patrick would be a wonderful representative for the value and worth found in every autistic individual, and I sensed he and I could advocate from experience to help meet the needs of autistic students and their families. Excitement and joy filled my heart.

"I love this idea!" I said. "And Patrick, you will bless that committee so much! I think you should do it," I said.

"I know. I already asked the Lord about it, and He said I should!" Patrick said.

With that focus, I knew the Lord was going to do amazing things in the days ahead.

So many times, when I face challenges and difficulties, I think the whole deal is all about me. It's not. Yes, Patrick's autism affected him and our family, but God had a greater plan. He intended to use it all along to bless others and to make them aware of Him. And that's exactly what He has been and is doing. Praise the Lord!

When I went to watch Patrick in a Glee Club performance his spring semester of freshman year (he joined that too), I sat directly behind Paula Morris, administrative assistant for Student Development. She had performed alongside Patrick as she also had a singing role in "Smoke on the Mountain." I leaned forward and said, "I just have to thank you for everything this university has meant to Patrick and our family."

"No, we are the ones who need to thank you, and Patrick," she said. "He is teaching all of us—students and faculty alike—so many wonderful things. We are fortunate to have him here. Thank you for sending him to us."

The Lord is so good!

Patrick's Perspective:

God gave me a great freshman year at Pfeiffer University. I prayed that I would not be lonely, and look what He did! He gave me lots of amazing friends! I know God made me autistic, and He has good plans with that. I really missed singing my first semester in college, so I was glad when I got to participate in Pfeiffer Idol and sing. I have been singing on campus since then. When I get to sing about how great God is and all the wonderful things He has done, it makes me especially happy. Looking back, I could not have imagined having such a great first year in college. I owe everything to God, and I hope I will always honor Him in the things I do.

SOMETHING TO THINK ABOUT:

Would you trust that God has great and

amazing plans for your life?

Would you cooperate with whatever the

Lord wants to do in and through you?

Would you see that life is not all about us, but about

Who God is and how He wants to move through our

lives to make Himself known?

How could God use the things you love to honor Him?

*Patrick's confidence grew after his many successes
during freshman year at Pfeiffer*

Patrick became a familiar face on the Pfeiffer Chapel's stage

Patrick performing in Smoke on the Mountain

28

COMING FULL CIRCLE

"He has made everything beautiful in its time."
—Ecclesiastes 3:11, NIV

When Patrick and I were about to speak at the Special Needs Mini-Conference in Salisbury, NC, we were interviewed by a writer from the local newspaper about our upcoming presentation and Patrick's life. The story ran on the front page of the *Salisbury Post* on April 29, 2012. Shortly thereafter, I received a phone call from the Women of Faith organization.

"Susan, we received a copy of the story that ran in the Salisbury Post newspaper," said the representative on the phone. "Could you tell me more about your experience at the Women of Faith conference?"

I recounted the entire story, filling in more details as I went. (The story is found in Chapter 3 of this book.) The young lady rejoiced alongside me as I narrated my personal account of God's faithfulness, and His power and love displayed through my son.

"That is an incredible story! Thank you for sharing it with me," she said. "And as a way of celebrating what God has done, we would like to offer you two free tickets to attend the Women of Faith conference, October 19-20, in Charlotte. We plan to seat you on the front row."

I was speechless, totally surprised by her words.

"Who was the speaker that day back in 1995?" she asked.

"Marilyn Meberg," I said.

"Wonderful! She will be one of the speakers in Charlotte. How would you and your guest like to meet her backstage during the conference? We would like to arrange that for you," she said.

"That would be incredible! Thank you so much! I have always wanted to thank her for how the Lord used her to help me. I had thought about writing her a letter. Thanking her in person would be so much better!" I said.

"Okay. Then it's settled," she said. "I will make all the arrangements, and we will be in touch soon."

The caller was true to her word, and the tickets arrived in the mail shortly thereafter. My daughter Katie was thrilled to accompany me to the event. I was sharing with my friend Becky at church about all that had transpired, and she quickly jumped in and convinced about 30 other ladies from church to attend the event. We joyously embarked for Charlotte together.

As I walked into Time Warner Cable Arena on October 19, I thought about how differently I felt that day, compared to 14 years ago. My heart was racing with joy as I joined the throng of women heading into the building. The pulsating praise music swept me into the electric atmosphere as an usher led Katie and me to the front row seats. As we sat down, I looked at the nearby stage, then at Katie, and tears filled my eyes. I was overwhelmed by the Lord's kindness, extended through His faithful servants at the Women of Faith organization.

I *LOVED* being there! The speakers shared profoundly from the Bible and their personal life experiences. The praise and worship team raised our spirits to praise and thank the Lord. And the Ballet Magnificat troupe used the forms of their agile bodies in combination with spectacular melodies to teach powerful spiritual truths.

Then there was Marilyn. She took the platform to share more Biblical wisdom with the same strength, humor, and tenderness I remembered from so many years ago. When the Women of Faith representative came to get Katie and me for our meeting with Marilyn backstage, I felt the excitement building inside me. The representative took us to a curtained-off area behind the back side of the arena. I noticed a large circle of chairs and intuitively knew that the Women of Faith staff gathered there to pray before their events. Soon, Marilyn entered the area.

Unable to contain my excitement, I leaped from my chair and

ran up to hug her.

"I am so happy to meet you," she said.

"And I am so happy to meet you!" I said.

I introduced Katie, and the three of us spent the next 15 minutes sharing the joy of the Lord.

Marilyn asked questions about Patrick and our family. She even asked Katie about how Patrick had impacted her life. I was touched by her sensitivity and genuine desire to learn more about us.

"I think the Lord has chosen to use Patrick to magnify Himself," Marilyn said.

I knew she was right!

"Marilyn, it is about time to start the next session," the Women of Faith representative said.

We snapped a few pictures, and I handed Marilyn a thank you letter I had written and a CD containing a copy of Patrick's sermon from Graduation/Youth Sunday. We hugged, and everyone departed to their places. The next session involved all the speakers, and Marilyn smiled and waved at me and as she walked onto the platform.

She is such a representative of Your grace, Lord, I prayed. *Thank You for allowing me to meet her in person. It was beyond what I ever could have asked for or imagined.*

As the praise team entered the platform for the final series of praise and worship songs, I praised and thanked the Lord over and over for what He had done.

When the Lord called Moses on Mount Horeb to go and deliver His people from slavery in Egypt, Moses hesitated, overwhelmed by his own personal inadequacies. God reminded Moses, "Certainly I will be with you, and this shall be the sign to you that it is I who have sent you: when you have brought the people out of Egypt, you shall worship God at this mountain (Exodus 3:12, NASB)."

My "mountain experience," where I faced my own inadequacies and realized the Lord was with me, was at the Women of Faith conference those many years ago. And now, the Lord had brought me back to the mountain, where I was worshipping Him! Joy and gratitude burst from my heart like a never-ending fountain.

Marilyn was right. The Lord had used Patrick—and would continue to do so—to magnify Himself.

David told me once that when he was going through his own personal struggle about being a father to Patrick and facing an uncertain future, that the Lord had told him, "He is My son, not yours. And I have made him to be an encouragement to believers and a light in an ever-darkening world." The Lord has given us the privilege and blessing of experiencing the fulfillment of those words.

When the disciple Paul faced his own personal weaknesses, the Lord told him, "My grace is sufficient for you, for My power is made perfect in weakness" (2 Corinthians 12:9a, NIV).

When he heard those words from the Lord, Paul replied, "Therefore I will boast all the more gladly about my weaknesses, so that Christ's power may rest on me. That is why, for Christ's sake, I delight in weaknesses, in insults, in hardships, in persecutions, in difficulties. For when I am weak, then I am strong" (2 Corinthians 12:9b-10, NIV).

When God says His grace is sufficient for us, He uses words in the original language of the Bible that refer to His favor, lovingkindness, and mercy being enough for any danger or trouble we face. When the scripture says, "For when I am weak, then I am strong," it literally means, "When I am weak [in human strength], then I am [truly] strong (able, powerful in divine strength)" (2 Corinthians 12:10b, Amp).

I saw the truth of those words in Patrick's life: his weakness, my weakness, and my family's weakness in dealing with autism had been used by God to show His enormous power and strength. Patrick's accomplishments stem from the power, love, and grace of God. The Lord moved in our weakness to display His glory. I agree with Paul: I want to rely on the power and grace of God, and not my own strength. I know the Lord has enough power and grace to see me through to the finish line, where I will praise Him forevermore!

Patrick's Perspective:

Look at what God has done through my autism. He took someone who could not talk and made them sing, someone who could not jump and made them swim, and someone who could not learn and sent them to college! If He could do that for me, just think about what He could do for you. Jesus loves all of us. That is what really matters. Because Jesus loves me, I want to live my life for Him. I hope I can show other people how much Jesus loves them through my life. I see what a difference knowing Jesus can make, and I hope other people can experience that, too. The Bible says, "Whatever you do, do it all for the glory of God" (1 Corinthians 10:31, NIV). That is what I want to do, and I know God will help me do it. He can help you do it, too!

SOMETHING TO THINK ABOUT:

How and where are you weak and inadequate? Would you thank God for those things, knowing they are the very place where He wants to display His power and grace?

Would you rely on the Lord's strength instead of your own, especially as you face your personal challenges?

Would you allow the Lord to use your weak places to display His glory?

How might the Lord want to reveal Jesus to others through you?

29

DANCING IN THE RAIN

"I shall give you rains in their season,
so that the land will yield its produce
and the trees of the field will bear their fruit."
—*Leviticus 26:4, NASB*

Have you ever seen children playing in the rain? They freely embrace and rejoice in the deluge falling upon them. Arms uplifted, they jump and stomp into puddles, splashing the water in every direction. Laughter and giggles mingle with the sound of raindrops hitting the leaves, grass, and pavement around them. They *love* the rain.

But, as we get older, when the rain shows up in our lives, we often resent it. We try not to get wet. We pop open an umbrella, rejecting the raindrops pouring from heaven. We see the rain as an inconvenience, spoiling our plans for the day, making driving more difficult, even threatening to soak our clothes and spoil our well-coiffed hair.

I resented the "rain" when we first received Patrick's diagnosis of autism. A storm had invaded my life, and I didn't want it. I saw his autism as an unwelcome tempest that threatened my dreams and my family. I tried to protect myself, my family, and especially my son from the downpour that threatened to engulf and sweep us away.

Now, I recognize the rain as good. That's because the Lord sent the rain. He allowed it for a beautiful purpose. It was sent to produce stunning and satisfying fruit. His presence permeates the rain like the sweet smell in the restorative rains that come every spring. Scripture tells us, "So let us know, let us press on to know the Lord. His going forth is as certain as the dawn, and he will come to us like the rain, like the spring rain watering the earth" (Hosea 6:3, NASB).

The Lord is good, and He intends the rain for good.

In my life, the rain drew me to Him and made me realize how much I needed Him. And He refreshed me with Himself. In the process, He purified me. The stuff that really wasn't all that important washed away. I experienced His love in newer and deeper ways, and it gave me the desire to live my life in a way that honors Him. The rain cleansed my life.

Suddenly, I realized that all of my longings, all the things I thought I needed are found in Him. He is the only source for quenching my thirst. I opened my life to receive Him, and He filled me up to overflowing. He makes the living water He gave me to spill out and over onto those around me, so they can see how beautifully satisfying He is. He leads me to respond to Him like the dry, parched ground, like shriveled leaves that soak in restorative streams of life. I grow. I bloom. I prosper. Because God sent the rain.

He brings fruit from the rain. He plants and cultivates, grows and harvests His best plans and purposes through the waters of adversity in my life. He produces miraculous wonders, and He uses the rain to do it!

Whatever the challenge or struggle, that rainstorm is something beautiful, sent by an all-loving, all-knowing Father, who only wants the best for us and for those around us.

Day by day, He allows us to see the gift. And before we realize it, we are dancing in the rain.

Patrick's Perspective:

For a long time, I did not like being autistic. There are still some things I do not like about it. But now, I look at my autism as something good. It is something the Lord has used to help others. I also have drawn closer to Him because of it. I trust that God will continue to use my autism in the future. Some people would say I am handicapped because I have autism, but I don't think I am handicapped. I think I would be handicapped if I didn't know Jesus.

SOMETHING TO THINK ABOUT:

What is your "rain"?

Will you place it on the altar, for God to

accomplish His purposes through it?

Will you trust God to use the rain for your

good and the good of others?

Would you anticipate that, in time,

you could be dancing in the rain?

Susan and Patrick have learned to thrive while living with autism (Photo by Karen Goforth)

SUSAN JANE KING

Want to See More About Patrick?
Check Out These Links:

(Most of these links can be found at
susanjaneking.com on the News page.)

"The Challenges and Blessings of Living with Autism" (Patrick and Susan's talks at the Special Needs Mini-Conference):
http://www.youtube.com/watch?v=2IoouSA9jaA&feature=youtu.be

"Integrity and Identity in Christ" (Patrick's sermon during Graduation/Youth Sunday):
http://www.youtube.com/watch?v=AkOz10O4VME

The Salisbury Post *newspaper story about Patrick and his autism:*
http://www.salisburypost.com/News/042912-patrick-king-from-autism-to-happily-ever-after-qcd

The Salisbury Post *newspaper story about Patrick signing with the Pfeiffer University Swim Team:*
http://www.salisburypost.com/Sports/042412-King-qcd

The Falcon's Eye *(Pfeiffer University student newspaper) story about Patrick winning Pfeiffer Idol (see page 10 in the newspaper):*
http://media.pfeiffer.edu/falconseye/Jan13.pdf

Patrick, doing the Harlem Shake, with his friends at Pfeiffer University:
http://www.youtube.com/watch?v=icVd1xZ7EUE&feature=youtu.be

SCRIPTURE VERSES BY CHAPTER

Bible Translation Guide:

Amp. = Amplified Bible
HCSB = Holman Christian Standard Bible
KJV = King James Version
NASB = New American Standard Bible
NCV = New Century Version
NIV = New International Version
NLT = New Living Translation

Chapter 1: What's Wrong?

"Oh, my anguish, my anguish! I writhe in pain. Oh, the agony of my heart!" —Jeremiah 4:19, NIV

"Children are a gift from the Lord." —Psalm 127:3, NLT

Chapter 2: A Maze of Tests

"Lord, You are my lamp; the Lord illuminates my darkness." —2 Samuel 22:29, HCSB

"God has said, 'Never will I leave you; never will I forsake you.'" —Hebrews 13:5, NIV

Chapter 3: "Your Son Has Autism"

"'For I know the plans I have for you,' declares the Lord, 'plans to prosper you and not to harm you, plans to give you hope and a future.'" —Jeremiah 29:11, NIV

"Lean on, trust in, and be confident in the Lord with all your heart and mind, and do not rely on your own insight or understanding. In all your ways know, recognize, and acknowledge Him, and He will direct and make straight and plain your paths." —Proverbs 3:5-6, Amp.

"Trust in Him at all times, O people; pour out your heart before Him; God is a refuge for us." —Psalm 62:8, NASB

Chapter 4: Talking

"By my God I can leap over a wall." —2 Samuel 22:30, NASB

"Nothing is impossible with God." —Luke 1:37, NLT

Chapter 5: Organizing the World

"There is a time for everything, and a season for every activity under the heavens." —Ecclesiastes 3:1, NIV

"The mind of man plans his way, but the Lord directs his steps." — Proverbs 16:9, NASB

"For God is not the author of confusion, but of peace." —1 Corinthians 14:33, KJV

Chapter 6: Walking in Patrick's Shoes

"Be sympathetic, love one another, be compassionate and humble." —1 Peter 3:8, NIV

"And we know that God causes all things to work together for good to those who love God, to those who are called according to His purpose." — Romans 8:28, NASB

"And my God will supply all your needs according to His riches in glory in Christ Jesus." —Philippians 4:19, NASB

Chapter 7: Quitting Work

"There is a time for everything, and everything on earth has its special season." —Ecclesiastes 3:1, NCV

"Yes, everything else is worthless when compared with the infinite value of knowing Christ Jesus my Lord. For His sake I have discarded everything else, counting it all as garbage, so that I could gain Christ." —Philippians 3:8, NLT

Chapter 8: Learning to Truly See Others

"Do nothing from selfishness or empty conceit, but with humility of mind regard one another as more important than yourselves; do not merely look out for your own personal interests, but also for the interests of others." —Philippians 2:3-4, NASB

"It is more blessed to give than to receive." —Acts 20:35, NASB

"Fixing our eyes on Jesus, the author and perfecter of faith, who for the joy set before Him endured the cross, despising the shame, and has sat down at the right hand of the throne of God." —Hebrews 12:2, NASB

Chapter 9: Choosing to be Thankful

"In everything give thanks; for this is God's will for you in Christ Jesus." —1 Thessalonians 5:18, NASB

"'For I know the plans that I have for you,' declares the Lord, 'plans for welfare and not for calamity to give you a future and a hope.'" —Jeremiah 29:11, NASB

"I will give thanks to You, for I am fearfully and wonderfully made; wonderful are Your works, and my soul knows it very well." —Psalm 139:14, NASB

SUSAN JANE KING

Chapter 10: Finding God in the Dark Times

"If I say, 'Surely the darkness will overwhelm me, and the light around me will be night,' even the darkness is not dark to You, and the night is as bright as the day. Darkness and light are alike to You." —Psalm 139:11-12, NASB

"It is by grace that you have been saved, and that is not of yourselves. It is a gift from God, not of works, so that no one may boast." —Ephesians 2:8-9, NASB

"These are the nations that the Lord left in the land to test those Israelites who had not experienced the wars of Canaan. He did this to teach warfare to generations of Israelites who had no experience in battle." —Judges 3:1-2, NLT

"I can do all things through Him who strengthens me." —Philippians 4:13, NASB

"But in all these things we overwhelmingly conquer through Him who loved us." —Romans 8:37, NASB

"God has said, 'Never will I leave you; never will I forsake you.' So we say with confidence, 'The Lord is my Helper; I will not be afraid. What can mere mortals do to me?'" —Hebrews 13:5-6, NIV

"I will be glad and rejoice in You; I will sing the praises of Your name, O Most High." —Psalm 9:2, NIV

"For the word of God is living and active and sharper than any two-edged sword, and piercing as far as the division of soul and spirit, of both joints and marrow, and able to judge the thoughts and intentions of the heart." — Hebrews 4:12, NASB

"The words that I have spoken to you are spirit and are life." —John 6:63, NASB

"And take the helmet of salvation, and the sword of the Spirit, which is the word of God." —Ephesians 6:17, NASB

"Why are you in despair, O my soul? And why are you disturbed within me? Hope in God, for I shall again praise Him, the help of my countenance and my God." —Psalm 43:5, NASB

"My soul waits in silence for God only; from Him is my salvation . . . My soul, wait in silence for God only, for my hope is from Him. He only is my rock and my salvation, my stronghold; I shall not be shaken. On God my salvation and my glory rest; the rock of my strength, my refuge is in God. Trust in Him at all times, O people; pour out your heart before Him; God is a refuge for us." —Psalm 62:1, 5-8, NASB

"This I recall to my mind, therefore I have hope. The Lord's lovingkindnesses indeed never cease, for His compassions never fail. They are new every morning; great is Your faithfulness. 'The Lord is my portion,' says my soul, 'Therefore I have hope in Him.' The Lord is good to those who wait for Him, to the person who seeks Him. It is good that he waits silently for the salvation of the Lord." —Lamentations 3:21-26, NASB

Chapter 11: Navigating the Marriage Waters

"For this cause a man shall leave his father and mother, and shall cleave to his wife; and the two shall become one flesh. This mystery is great; but I am speaking with reference to Christ and the church." —Ephesians 5:31-32, NASB

"Then God said, 'Let Us make man in Our image, according to Our likeness.'" —Genesis 1:26, NASB

"For we are His workmanship, created in Christ Jesus for good works, which God prepared beforehand so that we would walk in them." —Ephesians 2:10, NASB

"For by wise guidance you will wage war, and in abundance of counselors there is victory." —Proverbs 24:6, NASB

"Do not be deceived: 'Bad company corrupts good morals.'" —1 Corinthians 15:33, NASB

"Though one may be overpowered, two can defend themselves. A cord of

three strands is not quickly broken.” —Ecclesiastes 4:12, NASB

Chapter 12: Hiking the Trail to Manhood

“He told our fathers to teach their children.” —Psalm 78:5, NLV

“‘So do not fear, for I am with you; do not be dismayed, for I am your God. I will strengthen you and help you; I will uphold you with my righteous right hand.’” —Isaiah 41:10, NIV

“When I’m afraid, I will put my trust in You.” —Psalm 56:3, NASB

Chapter 13: Realizing God Works Wonders

“Who is like You among the gods, O Lord? Who is like You, majestic in holiness, awesome in praises, working wonders?” —Exodus 15:11, NASB

“Now to Him who is able to do far more abundantly than all that we ask or think, according to the power at work within us, to Him be glory in the church and in Christ Jesus throughout all generations, forever and ever. Amen.” —Ephesians 3:20-21, ESV

Chapter 14: Speaking Life Over Others

“Death and life are in the power of the tongue.” —Proverbs 18:21, NASB

“Let no unwholesome word proceed from your mouth, but only such a word as is good for edification, according to the need of the moment, so that it will give grace to those who hear.” —Ephesians 4:29, NASB

“Encourage one another day after day, as long as it is still called ‘Today.’” —Hebrews 3:13, NASB

Chapter 15: Refusing to Make Assumptions about People

"Man looks at the outward appearance, but the Lord looks at the heart."
—1 Samuel 16:7, NASB

"There is one lawgiver and judge who is able to save and to destroy. But who are you to judge your neighbor?" —James 4:12, HCSB

Chapter 16: Learning to Forgive

"And forgive us our debts, as we also have forgiven our debtors." —Matthew 6:12, NASB

"Bear with each other and forgive whatever grievances you may have against one another. Forgive as the Lord forgave you." —Colossians 3:13, NIV

"Please obey the Lord in what I am saying to you, that it may go well with you and you may live." —Jeremiah 38:20, NASB

Chapter 17: Encountering Love through Family and Friends

"God places the lonely in families." —Psalm 68:6, NIV

"Every good thing given and every perfect gift is from above, coming down from the Father of lights, with whom there is no variation or shifting shadow." —James 1:17, NASB

"In everything I did, I showed you that by this kind of hard work we must help the weak, remembering the words the Lord Jesus himself said: 'It is more blessed to give than to receive.'" —Acts 20:35, NIV

Chapter 18: Noticing the Details

"For since the creation of the world His invisible attributes, His eternal power and divine nature, have been clearly seen, being understood through what has been made." —Romans 1:20, NASB

"But now ask the beasts, and let them teach you; and the birds of the heavens, and let them tell you. Or speak to the earth, and let it teach you; and let the fish of the sea declare to you. Who among all these does not know that the hand of the Lord has done this, in whose hand is the life of every living thing, and the breath of all mankind?" —Job 12:7-10, NASB

"The heavens are telling of the glory of God; and their expanse is declaring the work of His hands. Day to day pours forth speech, and night to night reveals knowledge." —Psalm 19:1-2, NASB

Chapter 19: Determining to Keep Going with God

"Let us run with endurance the race that is set before us, fixing our eyes on Jesus, the author and perfecter of faith." —Hebrews 12:1-2, NASB

"I can do all things through Christ who strengthens me." —Philippians 4:13, NASB

Chapter 20: Being Welcomed to the Table

"He hath made us accepted in the beloved." —Ephesians 1:6, KJV

"But as many as received Him, to them He gave the right to become children of God, even to those who believe in His name." —John 1:12, NASB

"Then he said to me, 'Write, Blessed are those who are invited to the marriage supper of the Lamb.' And he said to me, 'These are true words of God.'" —Revelation 19:9, NASB

"Then she called the name of the Lord who spoke to her, 'You are a God who sees.'" —Genesis 16:13, NASB

Chapter 21: Driving

"Behold, I will do something new, now it will spring forth; will you not be aware of it? I will even make a roadway in the wilderness, rivers in the desert."

—Isaiah 43:19, NASB

Chapter 22: Leaving Your Problems at the Door

"Cast all your anxiety on Him because He cares for you." —1 Peter 5:7, NIV

"Why are you in despair, O my soul? And why have you become disturbed within me? Hope in God, for I shall yet praise Him, the help of my countenance and my God." —Psalm 42:11, NASB

"Therefore let us draw near with confidence to the throne of grace, so that we may receive mercy and find grace to help in time of need." —Hebrews 4:16, NASB

Chapter 23: Entering the Public Forum

"My mouth will speak the praise of the Lord, and all flesh will bless His holy name forever and ever." —Psalm 145:21, NASB

"Nothing is impossible with God" —Luke 1:37, NASB

I will exalt You, my God the King; I will praise Your name for ever and ever. Every day I will praise You and extol Your name for ever and ever. Great is the Lord and most worthy of praise; His greatness no one can fathom. One generation commends Your works to another; they tell of Your mighty acts. They speak of the glorious splendor of Your majesty—and I will meditate on Your wonderful works. They tell of the power of Your awesome works—and I will proclaim Your great deeds. They celebrate Your abundant goodness and joyfully sing of Your righteousness. The Lord is gracious and compassionate, slow to anger and rich in love. The Lord is good to all; He has compassion on all He has made. All Your works praise You, Lord; Your faithful people extol You. They tell of the glory of Your kingdom and speak of Your might, so that all people may know of Your mighty acts and the glorious splendor of Your kingdom. Your kingdom is an everlasting kingdom, and Your dominion endures through all generations. The Lord is trustworthy in all He promises and faithful in all He does. My mouth will speak in praise of the Lord. Let every creature praise His holy name for ever and ever. —Psalm 145:1-13, 21, NIV

Chapter 24: Walking through the Open Door

"Behold, I have put before you an open door which no one can shut." —Revelation 3:8, NASB

Chapter 25: Starting College

"You will keep in perfect peace all who trust in You, all whose thoughts are fixed on You!" —Isaiah 26:3, NLT

Chapter 26: Being Sharpened as Siblings

"Iron sharpens iron; so a man sharpens the countenance of his friend [to show rage or worthy purpose]." —Proverbs 27:17, Amp.

Chapter 27: Making a Big Splash

"No eye has seen, no ear has heard, and no mind has imagined what God has prepared for those who love Him." —1 Corinthians 2:9, NLT

Chapter 28: Coming Full Circle

"He has made everything beautiful in its time." —Ecclesiastes 3:11, NIV

"And He said, 'Certainly I will be with you, and this shall be the sign to you that it is I who have sent you: when you have brought the people out of Egypt, you shall worship God at this mountain.'" —Exodus 3:12, NASB

"My grace is sufficient for you, for My power is made perfect in weakness. Therefore I will boast all the more gladly about my weaknesses, so that Christ's power may rest on me. That is why, for Christ's sake, I delight in weaknesses, in insults, in hardships, in persecutions, in difficulties. For when I am weak, then I am strong." —2 Corinthians 12:9-10, NIV

"When I am weak [in human strength], then I am [truly] strong (able,

powerful in divine strength)." —2 Corinthians 12:10b, Amp.

"Whatever you do, do it all for the glory of God." —1 Corinthians 10:31, NIV

Chapter 29: Dancing in the Rain

"I shall give you rains in their season, so that the land will yield its produce and the trees of the field will bear their fruit." —Leviticus 26:4, NASB

"So let us know, let us press on to know the Lord. His going forth is as certain as the dawn, and He will come to us like the rain, like the spring rain watering the earth." —Hosea 6:3, NASB

ACKNOWLEDGEMENTS

My heart overflows with gratitude as I think of all the people who played a role in bringing this book to life.

Thank you everyone who ever told me, "You should write a book," and persisted long enough that I finally listened, especially Mom (Jane Mathie), my mother-in-law Sally King, Susan Shinn, and Su Krotchko.

Phyllis Keels, I never could have imagined how the Lord would use you and your writing class to begin the work on this book! Your wisdom, encouragement, and editorial comments are woven within these pages. I treasure your friendship.

Susan Shinn, you are an editor extraordinaire! Thank you for your profound skills, valuable insights, and continued encouragement. You helped me believe I could do this.

Stacey Parker, your proofreading firmed up and shaped my writing. You are a gift and treasure to me and the writing community.

Kimberly Rae and Brian Thigpen of Narrow Way Books, you are amazing! Your designs, formatting, editorial intuitions, and marketing insights have resulted in a beautiful book that I cherish. Thank you for your patience, kindness, and grace in working with me. I value your friendship and professionalism.

Sarah and David Bracho of Creativity & Creation Photography, thank you for spending time with me and Patrick on campus and gifting to us the beautiful resulting photography. Your images capture Patrick's spirit—and your profound talents. We treasure your friendship.

Karen Goforth and Irresistible Portraits, thank you for allowing us to use Patrick's early photos at no charge and donating your time and skills to reformat those photos for use in this book. You have photographed Patrick from the time he was born and have captured wonderful memories for us. You will always be part of our family!

Thanks also, Karen, for the beautiful author photos, and Leslie Denton, of Pura Vida Photography, for visiting the pool with us and capturing the amazing cover photos. Thanks, too, Leslie for reformatting our family snapshots so they could be used in this book.

To all my family members and friends who read early versions of the manuscript, thank you for standing by me and giving great input about the book.

David King, your love and strength carried me through this book publishing process, as they have throughout our marriage. Thank you for your constant support and editorial comments. You are wise and wonderful, and I love you! I am so glad we could do this together.

Katie, Emily, and Sarah, you are treasured gifts from God and intricately woven through the tapestry of this book. Your mama loves you!

Patrick, you are my beloved son. Thank you for being willing to open up your life for the world to see . . . because Jesus is there.

Jesus, You have blessed me exceedingly and abundantly beyond what I could ever ask or imagine. Nothing is impossible with You!

Susan

ABOUT SUSAN JANE KING

Susan Jane King is a wife to an amazing man named David, mom to four incredible gifts from God named Katie, Emily, Sarah, and Patrick, and mother-in-law to a super son-in-law named Curt. A published writer, inspirational speaker, and devoted Bible teacher, Susan lives in China Grove, North Carolina. She helps lead Covenant Ministries and teaches a weekly adult Sunday School class with an average attendance of 90 persons at First Baptist Church in Salisbury, NC. Since her life has been impacted by autism, Susan loves to encourage and assist others in the special needs community. Her greatest passion is to help others thrive in their relationship with Jesus in the midst of life's ongoing challenges and struggles. Susan's speaking engagements have placed her before special needs communities, teachers, and Christian audiences. She loves digging into the scriptures and sharing with others how Biblical truths can be applied to daily living. Susan has a bachelor of science in journalism degree from the Ohio University School of Journalism, where she was named the Outstanding Graduate of 1983. She worked in public relations, advertising, and marketing for 14 years prior to being called to quit work. When she is not speaking, teaching, or writing, she enjoys coaxing her extremely mellow golden retriever Grace outside for a walk in God's beautiful creation.

Website and Blogs: www.susanjaneking.com

ABOUT PATRICK KING

Patrick King currently attends Pfeiffer University in Misenheimer, NC, where he is majoring in computer information systems. He received both academic and athletic scholarships to attend the university, where he swims on the Varsity Men's Swim Team and sings every chance he gets. He serves on Pfeiffer's newly created Autism Center Committee. At home, he is son to David and Susan and brother to Katie, Emily, and Sarah. He was thrilled when another male joined the King clan, as his sister Katie recently married Curt Morgan. Diagnosed with autism at age five, Patrick overcame dire predictions to achieve major accomplishments academically, athletically, and socially. As a result, he enjoys helping others find hope and encouragement on the autism and special needs journey. As a powerful speaker, vocalist, and writer, he relishes the opportunity to encourage parents, inspire others, and thank teachers and coaches for their impact on his and other students' lives. Patrick is especially passionate about helping people know of the love, hope, and grace found in Jesus. When he is not studying, speaking, swimming, or singing, Patrick enjoys playing and designing video games.

BIBILIOGRAPHY

Bible references quoted in this book are from: BibleGateway. The Lockman Foundation, n.d. Web. <http://www.biblegateway.com/>.

[i] "Autism Spectrum Disorders (ASDs)." *Centers for Disease Control and Prevention*. N.p., n.d. Web. 28 March. 2014. <http://www.cdc.gov/ncbddd/autism/data.html>.

[ii] Kromberg, Jennifer. "The 5 Stages of Grieving the End of a Relationship." *Psychology Today*. N.p., 11 Sept. 2013. Web. 3 Feb. 2014. <http://www.psychologytoday.com/blog/inside-out/201309/the-5-stages-grieving-the-end-relationship>.

[iii] Blackaby, Henry T., and Claude V. King. *Experiencing God: Knowing and Doing the Will of God*. Nashville: LifeWay Press, 1990. Print.

[iv] Worthington, S., & Saldana, Z. (Actors). (2009). *Avatar* [Online video]. United States: 20th Century Fox. Retrieved February 3, 2014.

[v] Walmark, Allison Z. "Autism: Breaking Up is Hard to Do." *She Knows Parenting*. N.p., 7 Jan. 2013. Web. 4 Feb. 2014. <http://www.sheknows.com/parenting/articles/979701/autism-and-divorce-rates>.

[vi] Eldredge, John. *Wild at Heart*. Nashville: Thomas Nelson, Inc., 2001. Print.

[vii] Dobson, James. *Bringing Up Boys Participant's Guide*. Carol Stream, IL: Tyndale House, 2003. Print.

[viii] Ortega, Fernando. *Give Me Jesus*. Give Me Jesus. Compact Disc. Word Entertainment Inc. 1991.

[ix] Mathie, Jane. Personal interview. 11 Nov. 2012.

[x] Anderson, Eric. Personal interview. 11 Apr. 2013.

[xi] "Temple Grandin: Understanding Autism." *60 Minutes Overtime*. CBS. 21 Oct. 2011. Web. 5 Feb. 2014. <http://www.cbsnews.com/news/temple-grandin-understanding-autism/>.

[xii] Loizeaux. *Bible Companion Series*, Professional Edition. Neptune, NJ: Loizeaux Brothers, Inc., 2000. N. p. CD-ROM.

[xiii] Loizeaux. *Bible Companion Series,* Professional Edition. Neptune, NJ: Loizeaux Brothers, Inc., 2000. N. p. CD-ROM.

[xiv] Cottrell, Travis. "Forevermore (Psalm 145)". *Found*. Compact Disc.

Indelible Creative Group LLC. 2006.

[xv] Casting Crowns. "Already There". *Come to the Well*. Compact Disc. Provident Label Group LLC, a division of Sony Music Entertainment. 2011.

[xvi] Goodell, Kimberly. "Pfeiffer's New Superstar." *The Falcon's Eye* Jan. 2013 [*Misenheimer, NC*] : 10. Web. 12 Feb. 2014. <http://media.pfeiffer.edu/falconseye/Jan13.pdf>.

Made in the USA
Lexington, KY
18 July 2014